Bibliographies and
African Stu

James C. Armstrong, A

The Economies of East Africa

Tony Killick

G. K. HALL & CO., 70 LINCOLN STREET, BOSTON, MASS.

Library of Congress Cataloging in Publication Data

Killick, Tony.
The economies of East Africa.

Includes index.
1. Africa, East--Economic conditions--Bibliography.
I. Title.
Z7165.A42K54 [HC517.E2] 016.3309'67 76-4933
ISBN 0-8161-7916-6

This publication is printed on permanent/durable acid-free paper
MANUFACTURED IN THE UNITED STATES OF AMERICA

Preface

When I first set out to compile this bibliography I had hoped for truly comprehensive coverage, from year dot and including all published and unpublished works. It was soon quite obvious that limits had to be established. The objective of this work was therefore finally defined as being to offer a comprehensive coverage of all substantial printed English-language publications appearing since 1963. Despite this narrowing of the coverage I fear that we will have missed some items that ought to have been included, for which apologies are offered. As part compensation, we have gone outside the limits just defined to include a substantial number of mimeographed items that are publicly available, although the coverage in this case is rather random and far from complete. Confidential materials have been left out, as well as unpublished theses. Government publications of a routine nature (annual reports, quarterly digests, and the like) have been excluded but we have attempted to include all publicly-available official publications of a non-routine nature, such as reports of commissions of enquiry, development plans and special surveys. The search process was largely completed in June 1975. Given the time it takes for journals and books published outside East Africa to find their way to Nairobi, this means that our 1974 coverage is only partial, to say nothing of 1975.

The entries have been arranged according to the classification scheme presented on pages xxi-xxiv. As any such scheme involves certain artificial boundaries, a fairly detailed subject index has also been compiled. A relatively limited number of entries are not annotated. These relate to references we picked up from other sources but could not trace in Nairobi. In these cases it seemed better to include such information as we did have, rather than to drop them altogether. Fuller information on these would be gratefully received, together with details of any items we may have missed altogether.

A considerable number of obligations have been incurred during the course of this work. The largest of these is to Festus Munyasa and Raghbir Singh Deol, both of whom did trojan work as full-time research assistants. Without their diligence this project would never have been finished. Carrie Kibunja, Thomas Kibua and Melvina Sibale also provided valuable help; Angelika Handelman completed a difficult and

PREFACE

boring typing assignment with admirable speed and accuracy. Mary Kempe, Research Documentalist of I.D.S., provided much valuable help and advice; the other librarians of Nairobi were equally kind; my colleagues at the University offered both encouragement and information; and my wife Inge assisted me greatly with editorial work. Finally, my gratitude goes to the Ford Foundation and to the University of Nairobi for the financial support which made this project possible. I hope the finished product is worthy of all those who have contributed.

University of Nairobi
September, 1975.

Contents

Introduction

The volume of past research

When the idea of compiling this bibliography was first conceived a modest part-time scheme was envisaged, employing two students during a long vacation and finally comprising two hundred entries or so. After all, it had been decided not to go back beyond 1963, to restrict ourselves to English-language publications and to concentrate largely on printed items, as distinct from mimeographed materials. Moreover, we were dealing with countries only recently independent, two of whom had not had their own universities for long.

It did not take long to realise that these plans were too modest. In the end nearly a thousand entries and well over 600 authors and editors were identified; even so, there are bound to be some that we have missed.

So how much do we know about the economies of East Africa? In compiling this bibliography, we were impressed with the volume of past publications; in this respect East Africa compares favourably with West Africa. Although it is difficult to make reliable judgements on the quality of the output, it appears generally that the overall quality of the literature is comparable with what one would expect to find in any part of the world: some rubbish, some work of the highest calibre.

When one disaggregates the literature into the various subject-headings employed here, one finds that most contain only a small number of entries; there is a need for far more work in virtually every field. The coverage is patchy both by topic and by country and there are some particularly serious neglects. Even on those subjects which have been well explored effective knowledge is less than it should be because only rarely has an author sat down to read all that exists on a topic to produce a survey or synthesis that would bring a mass of research findings into a systematic framework reduced to manageable length.

These qualifications notwithstanding, the volume of the literature on the East African economies is impressively large and is growing at the rate of 80 to 100 new items each year, so it is worth looking for explanations for this large output. The most fundamental, of course, is the existence in each country of universities that have encouraged research and commanded international respect. In each of these, special institutions were created specifically to promote research in economics and related social sciences: the East African Institute of Social Research at Makerere, the Economic Research Bureau at Dar-es-Salaam, and the Institute for Development Studies at Nairobi. Over the years each of these has been directly responsible for a large part of the literature recorded in this bibliography. They have also had positive indirect effects, for there are external economies in this business of research, with each researcher benefiting from, and building upon, the work that has already been done.

Ease of publication acts as another stimulus to research. Each of the institutes mentioned above has its own series of (usually) mimeographed research papers. But most authors aspire to something more permanent than that and in East Africa they have been blessed with the active presence of branches of several major 'multinational' publishing houses; the East African Literature Bureau (an agency of the Community); and the East African Publishing House. All of these can boast lengthy lists of works relating to the local economies, and the availability of these outlets has increased the attractiveness of research. The impressive research activities of the African Studies Centre of the IFO-Institut für Wirtschaftsforschung of Munich have contributed significantly to the literature contained in the bibliography, although they have now fallen sadly upon hard financial times.

Another facet of the same point has been the availability and growth in social science journals specialising in Eastern Africa or Africa as a whole: the _Eastern Africa Economic Review_, the _East African Journal of Rural Development_, the _Journal of Eastern African Research and Development_, the _Journal of Modern African Studies_, to name only some out of a rather extensive list of periodicals. The availability of these plus the proven willingness of various foreign-based academic journals to publish the results of economic research on East Africa (_See_ the List of Principal Journals, pp. xix-xx) means that few significant contributions need go unpublished; the problem for some editors may rather be one of maintaining standards.

Non-university institutions have also had a potent impact. East African governments have had a strong influence, both through their contacts with the universities and the research institutions mentioned earlier (very close in Tanzania, less intimate in Kenya, presumably rather remote in present-day Uganda) and through their ability to establish commissions of enquiry and the like. Several major entries in this bibliography are reports to government, which at their best can involve genuine research and substantially extend our knowledge of the local economy and its problems. Official statistical agencies are also potentially important, not only as providers of raw data but also for their own writings. Of the three countries,

Introduction

Kenya's Bureau of Statistics features most prominently on the pages of the bibliography as a source of several valuable contributions; the Community's Statistical Department has also initiated good work over the years and has commissioned a variety of articles for its own Economic and Statistical Review.

Reports by international agencies have had substantial impact as well. Two examples are the 1963 World Bank report on the economy of Kenya (entry 01-3), which stimulated a number of other contributions, and, even more important, the 1972 I.L.O. report on employment, incomes and equality in Kenya (entry 63-15). This is proving a work of major influence, not so much for the original material it contains, but rather for bringing much existing material together and putting it into a strong interpretive mould. In fact, this report provides a good example of the genuine contribution that can be made by a publication which is essentially synthetical in nature.

The 'research environment' has been another, not always positive, influence on the output of research. This especially has to do with the attitude of governments towards researchers and their work but is also influenced by the attitudes of other institutions, the general public, of potential funding agencies and of university administrations. That virtually nothing has been done on the economy of Zanzibar is presumably explicable in these terms, as is the paucity of work on recent developments in the economy of Uganda.

It unfortunately remains true that research on the East African economies is still largely done by non-Africans. Of the 646 individual authors and editors mentioned in the bibliography only 87, or 13 percent, were Africans, to judge from their names. Africanisation is occurring, however. Of the 50 publications which appeared in 1963 there was only one African author (to which we might dubiously add the names of the Chairmen of two committees which published reports to government); out of 97 entries for 1974-75, on the other hand, there were 24 African names.

Questions of balance, relevance and responsiveness

Imagine a regression analysis whose purpose is to explain the composition of past research on the East African economies. What variables might have significant explanatory power? Specifically, to what extent could the research output be attributed to the self-interests of researchers and to what extent to attempts to respond to the perceived needs of society and its government?

Both motivations enter into it, of course. The impression one gains from the works described in this bibliography is that among the more important influences on the choice of research topics should be included:

a. Academic acceptability, a consideration which provides some assurance as to the quality of the output and the rigour of its presentation but could carry the danger of conflict with a desire for socially relevant research.

b. Convenience and manageability. If researchers are optimisers they seek maximum outputs from given inputs. They may thus tend to choose topics which are conveniently manageable within a given time and other resources--hardly an unreasonable criterion but one which sometimes results in the choice of 'mini-micro' topics which may contribute rather little to a broader understanding of the economies and their problems unless they can subsequently be related to the broader context. A case in point is the strong bias in fiscal studies towards topics on local government finance: nicely manageable, no doubt, but of small economic significance. At least from this point of view, teamwork research is more likely to produce important results than individual efforts.

c. Responsiveness. It does not seem to me that the economics profession can be validly accused of having been excessively 'academic' or unresponsive to East African needs. The bibliography contains few titles which smack of academic boon-doggling, and a rather large proportion of titles of obvious relevance to local problems. Responsiveness, though, has its limitations. It is a passive concept: show us your needs and we will try to meet them. What the profession could more reasonably be criticised for is that it has been better at responding to felt needs than at anticipating them, except in certain specific fields such as population, education and rural development.

However responsive it may have been, the resulting body of literature, considered overall, is an unplanned consequence of atomistic research decisions. It is hardly surprising, therefore, that it contains gaps and biasses. One bias has already been mentioned: towards mini-micro studies. In the example of fiscal studies, no less than nine out of 24 entries under the heading of 'public finance and budgeting' (code 20) concern local government finance, despite the economic insignificance of local government in East Africa. Note also from the statistical summary on pp. xvii-xx that the subject headings with the largest numbers of entries were codes 41 and 42, dealing with studies of individual farms, or localities, or crops. A lot of the numerous entries under rural development (code 47) and the distributive system (code 56) are similarly local or narrow in their orientation.

The rural economy, indeed, has received a relatively massive coverage. So far as research is concerned, it is not true that the rural areas have been neglected. Indeed, one could argue that they have received disproportionate attention, to the neglect of numerous non-rural topics, although there still remain serious gaps in our knowledge of the rural economy, especially the semi-arid medium- or low-potential zones. Another subject-area which has received very extensive coverage is manpower planning and education (codes 64 and 70), with no less than 71 entries between them.

Compared with these areas of concentration there have been some serious neglects. Industry (broadly defined) and non-rural service activities have received nothing like the same attention as their rural counterparts, even granting the smaller importance of these sectors. Compare, for example the 101 farm, locality and crop studies (codes 41, 42) with the 14 entries under 'industry studies' (code 52).

Stabilisation and economic management is a particularly glaring and serious area of neglect, since all three countries now have serious balance of payments and inflationary problems. There are just two entries under code 15, 'domestic economic fluctuations and forecasting; inflation' (both of these relate to price controls in Tanzania) and three under code 32, 'balance of payments experiences and policies' (only one of which could be described as a substantial study). There is nothing on short-term economic forecasting, nothing on inflationary processes, hardly anything on macro-economic fiscal and monetary management.

Other neglected areas which suggest themselves include:

a. The relative lack of serious academic interest in statistical topics. The various official statistical agencies have produced a number of publications describing methods and setting out results but these have provoked little by way of response from the academic community.

b. The economics of the public sector. Since independence the size and importance of the public sector--the central government and para-statal agencies--has grown very considerably but only limited work has so far been done on the economics of this, and on relationships between the public and private sectors.

c. What can loosely be called social economics. I especially have in mind here the relative absence from the bibliography of studies of poverty (only one entry), nutrition (four entries) and drought (two entries). The social services, actual or potential, have similarly attracted only limited attention.

d. The markets for land and capital. By comparison with the very substantial literature on various aspects of the labour market, we know very little about the markets for rural or urban land, urban housing, and capital. There is, for example, no study of urban moneylenders; very few saving or investment studies; nothing on Kenya's stock exchange; and so on.

Introduction

To what extent, and in what directions, have the interests of researchers been changing over time? To answer this question an analysis was undertaken of publications that appeared respectively in 1963, 1969 and 1974-75. The broadest trend to stand out was for micro-economic studies to gain in prominence at the expense of macro studies, as shown below (figures are percentages of the total number of publications in the year in question):

	1963	1969	1974/75
Macro-economic (main codes 0 to 3, 6 and sub-code 80)	54	46	42
Micro-economic (main codes 4, 5, 7 and sub-code 81)	46	54	58
	100	100	100

Particular growth points included agricultural locality studies, income distribution and unemployment, foreign investment and aid. Also, it was in the latter half of the period that researchers discovered industry and the distributive system.

There has, on the other hand, been a fall in interest in development planning, and the more recent works on this tend to put more stress on implementation, less on methodology. Questions of land use, resettlement and tenure seem to be going out of fashion, as also the population issue. With the withdrawal of Newlyn's stimulus at the end of the sixties, there has been a fall-off in money and banking studies. And the malaise that affects the East African Community has infected would-be researchers too, with the notable exception of Hazlewood. Only a few substantial pieces have been written on the Community in the seventies, compared with a much greater output in earlier times.

It is not entirely self-evident that the trends just described represent an optimal adjustment to changing needs, as will be indicated shortly.

Country coverages and comparisons

Turning now to look at the research output in terms of country coverage, Kenya has attracted a very high proportion of the total research recorded here and Uganda has been seriously neglected (See statistical summary on pp. xxi-xxiv). Of the 676 country-specific entries, no fewer than 55 per cent related to Kenya and only 17 per cent to Uganda, with Tanzania claiming the remaining 28 per cent. These shares are quite out of proportion to the relative sizes and incomes of the three economies, as is clear from the following statistics, which relate to 1970:

	% of total EA population	% of total EA GDP	per capita incomes (shs)
Kenya	33	39	934
Tanzania	38	30	637
Uganda	29	31	870

It is likely that in some measure the specially strong showing of Kenya is a statistical artefact resulting because the bibliography was compiled exclusively in Nairobi. On the other hand, we did seek to guard against this bias as much as possible and my own judgement is that it can explain no more than a modest part of the disproportionate Kenyan coverage. It does not at all explain why Uganda should have a much weaker coverage than Tanzania. The longer traditions and initially wider reputation of Makerere University might have led one to expect the bias to be rather in favour of Uganda, but, of course, the research environment has scarcely encouraged fundamental enquiries there in recent years.

Turning now to look at each country in turn, the enormously greater research coverage of Kenya is reflected in virtually all subjects. It is particularly strong, however, on subjects relating to the rural economy, population and manpower, and social economics. It quite dominates the overall coverage of population studies, income distribution, employment and unemployment, the economics of education, and tourism. Coverage of its service industries and of para-statal agencies is relatively weak.

Strong points in the coverage of Tanzania provide a nice illustration of researchers' responsiveness to the circumstances of the economies they work in. Studies in political-economy, national and regional planning, public corporations, and rural development feature prominently, and the distributive system has also received a good deal of attention. On the other hand, issues in public finance, industry, population, employment and social policy remain little explored. And in Zanzibar there is virgin territory for the researcher. The bibliography lists only three entries on Zanzibar (despite a specially mounted search to find more): one is a government publication on the fruits of the revolution (entry 02-13), there is a brief article by Khamis (entry 10-71), and a 1963 household expenditure study. Nothing serious on the effects of the revolution, on the union with Tanganyika, or on the clove industry.

The coverage of Uganda is weak in nearly all departments. A fair amount has been done on money and credit, and on the distributive system, but it is much easier to point out topics on which very little has been published. There are, for example, no entries at all under the headings of 'general surveys' and 'political economy'; there is nothing on general development strategies and development administration; nothing on international trade. And while for East Africa as a whole the rural economy has received disproportionate attention, this could not be said of Uganda. Looking at the statistical summary one is struck by the small number of entries under locality studies (code 41), agricultural development (code 43), extension (code 46) and rural development (code 47). A particularly noticeable, if unsurprising, neglect is the absence of virtually any discussion of the post-Obote period and of Amin's 'economic war'. The reasons for this are obvious but regrettable none the less, for there are surely important lessons to be learned from this innovation.

One could sum up the foregoing by saying that there has been a lot of research but that it has been unplanned and has thus covered the ground less well than it could have done. There is thus a need for a conscious East African research strategy. Unfortunately, the Community is scarcely in a state to articulate one--although it could provide a valuable service by establishing an information storage and retrieval system--so that if strategies are to be defined it will have to be done at the national level. All three governments have at one time or another initiated moves in this direction. However, one suspects that in practice none of them has yet been able to formulate a meaningful strategy, even though a carefully worked-out set of priorities would promote an improved allocation of research resources.

What is especially important is that future research efforts should go beyond the task of filling gaps in our knowledge in order to *anticipate* the emergence of new problems. In this way, future work could better serve the needs of society, as well as satisfy the aspirations of researchers and their institutions.

List of Abbreviations

Afr Rev	*African Review*
EAER	*Eastern Africa Economic Review*
EAJ	*East Africa Journal*
EAJ Rural Devel	*East African Journal of Rural Development*
Econ Bull Afr	*Economic Bulletin for Africa*
Econ Dev Cult Change	*Economic Development and Cultural Change*
Econ Stat Rev	*Economic and Statistical Review*
ERB	Economic Research Bureau, University of Dar-es-Salaam
FAO	United Nations Food and Agriculture Organisation
IDS	Institute for Development Studies, University of Nairobi
IDS Disc P	*IDS Discussion Paper* (occasional series)
IFO	Institut für Wirtschaftsforschung Munich (Publishers: Weltforum Verlag, Munich)
J Admin Overseas	*Journal of Administration Overseas*
J Comm Mkt Stud	*Journal of Common Market Studies*
J Dev Areas	*Journal of Developing Areas*
J Dev Studs	*Journal of Development Studies*
J Mod Afr Studs	*Journal of Modern African Studies*
K Stat Dig	*Kenya Statistical Digest*
OECD	Organization for Economic Cooperation and Development, Paris
OIES Bull	*Bulletin of Oxford Institute of Economics and Statistics*
SRDP	Special Rural Development Programme (Kenya)
UN	United Nations Organization
UNESCO	United Nations Educational, Scientific and Cultural Organization, Paris

List of Principal Journals and Publishers

Title	Publication details
African Affairs	Royal Africa Society, London
African Economic History Review (mimeo)	University of Wisconsin
African Review	East Africa Literature Bureau, Nairobi
African Studies Review	African Studies Center, Michigan
African Urban Notes	African Studies Center, Michigan
Bulletin of Oxford Institute of Economics and Statistics	Basil Blackwell, Oxford
Canadian Journal of African Studies	Canadian Association of African Studies, Toronto
Development and Change	Institute of Social Studies, The Hague
East African Geographical Review	Uganda Geographical Association and Makerere University, Kampala
East Africa Journal	East African Publishing House, Nairobi
East African Agriculture and Forestry Journal (mimeo)	East African Agriculture and Forestry Research Organisation, Nairobi
East African Journal of Rural Development	East African Agricultural Economics Society and Makerere University, Kampala
East African Economic Review	East Africa Literature Bureau, Nairobi (formerly Oxford University Press, Nairobi)
Economic Bulletin for Africa	U.N. Economic Commission for Africa, U.N. Publications, New York
Economic Development and Cultural Change	University of Chicago Press, Chicago
Economic and Statistical Review	East African Statistical Department, Nairobi

List of Principal Journals and Publishers

Journal	Publisher
Hadith (occasional)	East African Publishing House for Historical Association of Kenya, Nairobi
IDS Discussion Papers (occasional series)	Institute for Development Studies, University of Nairobi
International Labour Review	International Labour Office, Geneva
Journal of Administration Overseas	Her Majesty's Stationery Office, London
Journal of Agricultural Economics	Agricultural Economics Society, Reading
Journal of Common Market Studies	Basil Blackwell, Oxford
Journal of Developing Areas	Western Illinois University
Journal of Development Studies	Cass & Co., London
Journal of East African Research and Development	East Africa Literature Bureau, Nairobi
Journal of Modern African Studies	Cambridge University Press, London
Kenya Statistical Digest	Central Bureau of Statistics, Nairobi
Uchumi	The Economics Society of Tanzania, Dar-es-Salaam
Uganda Journal	Uganda Society Publications, Kampala

Classification Scheme and Statistical Summary of Results

(Numbers refer to totals of individual entries.)

Code		Kenya	Tanzania	Uganda	Totals
0 - GENERAL STUDIES					
00	Historical and biographical studies	9	2	2	20
01	General surveys, comparative studies	3	2	-	11
02	Political economy, economic independence	4	7	-	13
03	Bibliographies, research programmes	4	1	-	20
	Sub-totals	20	12	2	64
1 - ECONOMIC DEVELOPMENT, PLANNING AND STABILISATION					
10	Growth and development: measurement and experiences	2	4	1	12
11	General development strategies and policies	4	4	-	9
12	Development planning and implementation	8	10	5	31
13	Macro-economic models	5	1	1	10
14	Public and development administration	9	6	-	18
15	Domestic economic fluctuations and forecasting; inflation	-	2	-	2
16	Consumption and saving studies	7	4	3	16
	Sub-totals	35	31	10	98

Note: The country statistics do not add up to the overall totals because of entries referring to more than one of the countries or to East Africa as a whole.

Classification Scheme and Statistical Summary of Results

Code		Kenya	Tanzania	Uganda	Totals
2 - FISCAL AND FINANCIAL TOPICS					
20	Public finance and budgeting	13	3	4	24
21	Domestic financial institutions and markets; money and credit	12	5	7	36
22	Domestic fiscal, financial and monetary policies	3	4	1	12
	Sub-totals	28	12	12	72
3 - INTERNATIONAL TRADE AND PAYMENTS: EAST AFRICAN CO-OPERATION					
30	International trade and trade relations; terms of trade	3	1	-	14
31	Commercial policies	1	2	-	9
32	Balance of payments experiences and policies	1	3	-	4
33	Foreign investments and aid	8	5	4	24
34	East African co-operation: general and historical	-	-	-	13
35	The East African Community	-	-	-	26
	Sub-totals	13	11	4	90
4 - THE AGRICULTURAL SECTOR					
40	Structure and organisation	2	-	1	7
41	Sample, locality and farm studies	26	15	4	49
42	Crop and livestock studies and policies	20	8	8	53
43	Agricultural development experiences	6	6	2	18
44	Agricultural strategies and planning	9	5	4	25
45	Land use, resettlement and tenure	23	5	6	42
46	Agricultural extension, technologies, price policies	8	1	2	16
47	Rural and community development, Ujamaa	11	17	1	36
48	Economic geography, natural resources, conservation, pollution	2	1	2	11
	Sub-totals	107	58	30	257

Classification Scheme and Statistical Summary of Results

Code		Kenya	Tanzania	Uganda	Totals
5 - THE INDUSTRIAL AND SERVICE SECTORS					
50	Industrial structure and organisation	13	3	1	17
51	Industrialisation, import substitution	4	1	1	9
52	Industry studies	3	1	2	14
53	Entrepreneurship; business finance and administration	2	-	-	7
54	Policies towards industry and private business	3	1	-	7
55	Transport and communications	1	2	2	9
56	Marketing, trading, co-operatives	10	10	11	45
57	Tourism	7	1	-	13
58	Public corporations and other para-statals	1	6	2	12
	Sub-totals	44	25	19	133
6 - POPULATION, MANPOWER, TECHNOLOGIES					
60	Demographic characteristics, population growth and development, population policies	18	2	4	34
61	The labour force; migration	6	7	3	20
62	Productivity, incomes, industrial relations	16	4	3	26
63	Employment and unemployment; labour-intensity, the choice of techniques	24	-	6	32
64	Manpower and educational planning; Africanisation	9	6	6	28
	Sub-totals	73	19	22	140
7 - SOCIAL ECONOMICS					
70	Economics of education	23	6	6	43
71	Health, housing, water, social policy	12	4	4	22
72	Regional and urban planning and policies	7	6	1	17
	Sub-totals	42	16	11	82

Code		Kenya	Tanzania	Uganda	Totals
8 - ECONOMIC STATISTICS					
80	General and macro-economic statistical publications	6	3	3	22
81	Micro-economic statistical publications	6	2	-	10
	Sub-totals	12	5	3	32
	GRAND TOTALS	374	189	113	968

The Economies of East Africa

0 - GENERAL STUDIES

00 - Historical and biographical studies

00-1 ALPERS, E. A. The East African Slave Trade. East African Publishing House, Nairobi, 1967.
A critique of Coupland's interpretation of the history of the East African slave trade.

00-2 BRETT, E. A. Colonialism and Underdevelopment in East Africa. Heinemann, London, 1973, 330 pp.
Compares political and economic issues, and argues that in 1919-39 economic debates on railways, tariffs and marketing policies, rather than political questions, were of the greater importance for the future of East Africa.

00-3 BURKE, FRED G. Tanganyika: Preplanning. Syracuse University Press, New York, 1965, 108 pp.
A study of the historical development of planning in Tanganyika between 1921 and 1961.

*00-4 CAREY-JONES, N. S. 'The decolonisation of the white highlands of Kenya'. Geographical Journal, 1965, No. 2, pp. 186-201.

00-5 CONE, L. WINSTON and LIPSCOMB, J. F., eds. The History of Kenya Agriculture. University Press of Africa, Nairobi, 1972, 160 pp.
An integrated collection of essays covering 1896-1967.

00-6 FREDERICK, K. D. 'The role of market forces and planning in Uganda's economic development, 1900-1938'. EAER, June 1969, pp. 47-62.
Argues that the colonial government directed resources primarily into an area complementary to the interests of the mother country, and this was not optimal for Uganda's long-term development.

00-7 KIMAMBO, ISARIA N. 'The economic history of the Kamba, 1850-1950'. Hadith, No. 2, 1970, pp. 79-103.
Provides a critical synthesis of past writings and raises questions for future research.

THE ECONOMIES OF EAST AFRICA

GENERAL STUDIES

00-8 LIEBENOW, J. GUS. Colonial Rule and Political Development in Tanzania: The Case of Makonde. East African Publishing House, Nairobi, 1971, 360 pp.
Describes the external forces that have impinged on Makonde society and assesses their essentially negative impact on political, social and economic development.

00-9 MURIUKI, GODFREY. 'Kikuyu reaction to traders and British administration, 1850-1904'. Hadith, No. 1, 1968, pp. 101-18.
A largely descriptive account.

00-10 ODINGA, OGINGA. Not yet Uhuru: A Biography. Heinemann, London, 1967, 323 pp.
A summary of political beliefs. Argues that independence is undermined by neo-colonialism.

00-11 SHERIFF, ABDUL H. 'Dynamics of change in pre-colonial East African societies'. African Economic History Review, Fall 1974, pp. 7-13.
A discussion of the appropriateness of Boserup's analysis of relationships between population growth and agricultural change to the East African case.

00-12 SUTTON, J. E. G. Early Trade in Eastern Africa. East African Publishing House, Nairobi, 1973, 42 pp.
Offered as a conspectus and discussion of the present state of knowledge of trade, industry and production in Eastern Africa from the early iron age to the nineteenth century.

00-13 TURTON, E. R. 'The Isaq Somali diaspora and poll-tax agitation in Kenya, 1936-41'. African Affairs, July 1974, pp. 325-46.
Discusses the campaign of Isaac Somali for higher status in Kenya by paying higher taxes.

00-14 VAN ZWANENBERG, ROGER. The Agricultural History of Kenya. East African Publishing House, Nairobi, 1972, 56 pp.
Argues the view that Kenya's agriculture was developed by the British to produce export goods, with resources and growth deliberately concentrated on the settler-owned estate farms.
See also article in Hadith No. 4, 1972.

00-15 _____. Colonial Capitalism and Labour in Kenya, 1919-39. East African Literature Bureau, Nairobi, 1972.
Focuses on the methods employed to secure short-term African migrant labour onto European farms.

00-16 _____. 'The development of peasant commodity production in Kenya, 1920-40'. Economic History Review, Aug. 1974, pp. 442-54.
Examines factors encouraging agricultural production for the market.

00-17 WOLFF, RICHARD D. The Economics of Colonialism: Britain and Kenya, 1895-1930. Yale University Press, New Haven, 1969, 239 pp.
Argues that colonial policy in Kenya was a rational response to Britain's economic problems, from which she derived considerable advantage.

00-18 WRIGLEY, C. C. Crops and Wealth in Uganda: A Short Agrarian History. Oxford University Press, Kampala, 1970, 84 pp.
Covers 1890 to mid-1950s.

00-19 YOSHIDA, MASAO. 'The protected development of European agriculture in Kenya before the second world war'. EAJ Rural Devel, 1969, No. 2, pp. 77-102.
Argues that protection by high import tariffs and preferential railway tariffs throughout the interwar period led to increased production of some crops but caused interterritorial disputes.

00-20 YOSHIDA, M. and BELSHAW, D. Introduction of the Trade Licensing System for Primary Products in East Africa, 1900-1939. Mimeographed. East African Institute of Social Research Conference Proceedings, Jan. 1965, 29 pp.
A study of government intervention in the marketing of agricultural produce in East Africa.

01 - General surveys; comparative studies

01-1 BELL, PHILIP W., ed. African Economic Problems. 5 vols. Mimeographed. Makerere University, Kampala, 1964. 458.
A collection of published and unpublished works, with special reference to the problems of East Africa, intended for use by first year students. Vol. 1: Economic Ends, Means and Constraints, 372 pp.; Vol. 2: Production, Consumption and Work, 451 pp.; Vol. 3*: Growth and Change: Basic Determinants, 293 pp.; Vol. 4*: Growth and Change: Issues in Planning, 371 pp.; (fifth volume not traced).
*with Katherine H. Bell.

01-2 East African Institute of Social and Cultural Affairs. Problems of Economic Development in East Africa. East African Publishing House, Nairobi, 1965, 107 pp.

THE ECONOMIES OF EAST AFRICA

GENERAL STUDIES

(East African Institute)
Papers on economic planning, manpower, regional development, monetary and fiscal problems.

01-3 International Bank for Reconstruction and Development. The Economic Development of Kenya. Johns Hopkins Press, Baltimore, 1963, 380 pp.
An economic survey mission report reviewing the economic potential of Kenya, with recommendations to assist planning for the period to 1967.
See also entry 01-5 for Kenya government response.

01-4 International Monetary Fund. Surveys of African Economies, Vol. 2. IMF, Washington, 1969, 448 pp.
General surveys of East African economies, including substantial treatment of East African co-operation and the Community.

*01-5 Kenya, Republic of. Observations on the Report of an Economic Survey Mission from the International Bank for Reconstruction and Development. Government Printer, Nairobi, 1963, 20 pp.
See also entry 01-3.

01-6 McWILLIAM, M. D. 'Notes on "The Economic Development of Kenya"'. EAER, June 1963, pp. 13-21.
Comments on the I.B.R.D. report.
See entry 01-3.

01-7 ROBSON, P. and LURY, D. A. The Economies of Africa. Allen & Unwin, London, 1969, 528 pp.
Includes "The East African Economies: Kenya, Uganda and Tanzania" by B. van Arkadie and D. Ghai. A comparative general survey of the three East African economies.

01-8 RUTMAN, G. L. The Economy of Tanganyika. Praeger, New York, 1968, 190 pp.
Examines the government's efforts to increase Tanganyika's growth rate and the Africanisation of the political-economic system.

01-9 SMITH, HADLEY E., ed. Readings on Economic Development and Administration in Tanzania. Oxford University Press, London, 1966, 598 pp.
A collection of materials covering most major aspects of the economy. Intended as a first step towards meeting the need for a textbook on the Tanzanian economy.

01-10 No Entry.

01-11 WHETHAM, EDITH H. and CURRIE, JEAN I., eds. *Readings in the Applied Economics of Africa*. 2 vols. Cambridge University Press, 1967, Vol. 1: 216 pp.; Vol. 2: 228 pp.
Reproduces a variety of readings on East Africa. All of those which were published since 1963 have separate entries in this bibliography.

01-12 ZAJADACS, PAUL, ed. *Studies in Production and Trade in East Africa*. Weltforum Verlag, Munich, 1970, 452 pp.
Collection of analyses of the industrial sectors, trade, crafts and small-scale industries, and the role of marketing boards.

02 - Political economy; economic independence

02-1 ARRIGHI, GIOVANNI and SAUL, JOHN S. *Essays on the Political Economy of Africa*. Monthly Review Press, New York, 1973, 416 pp.
Includes: Saul, John S., 'African Socialism in One Country: Tanzania'. Surveys achievements, conditioning factors, contradictions and prospects.

02-2 BERG-SCHLOSSER, DIRK. *The Distribution of Income and Education in Kenya: Causes and Potential Political Consequences*. Weltforum Verlag, Munich, 1970, 80 pp.
Analyses the social and economic bases of politics in Kenya.

*02-3 BHAGWAN, M. R. 'Problems of socialist development in Tanzania'. *Monthly Review*, May 1972, pp. 28-39.

02-4 BIENEN, HENRY. *Tanzania: Party Transformation and Economic Development*. Princeton University Press, Princeton, 1967, 446 pp.
Relates economic and political development by showing how the ruling party interacts with the economy it undertakes to transform.

02-5 GHAI, DHARAM P., ed. *Economic Independence in Africa*. East African Literature Bureau, Nairobi, 1973, 235 pp.
Collection of papers presented at the Conference of Directors of Social and Economic Research Institutes in Africa (1971). Includes: Van Arkadie, Brian, 'Development of the State Sector and Economic Independence'; Kamau, C. M., 'Localising Capitalism: The Kenya Experience'.

GENERAL STUDIES

02-6 HELLEINER, G. K. 'Socialism and economic development in Tanzania'. J Dev Studs, Jan. 1972, pp. 183-204.
An analysis of "socialist" policies and their effects on short-term growth.

02-7 Kenya, Republic of. African Socialism and its Application to Planning in Kenya. Government Printer, Nairobi, 1969, 56 pp.
An important official statement of philosophy and development strategy, as derived from the theory of democratic African socialism.

02-8 LEYS, COLIN, ed. Politics and Change in Developing Countries. Cambridge University Press, 1969, 289 pp.
Includes: 'The economics of ideology: some problems of achieving rural socialism in Tanzania' by David Feldman.

02-9 LEYS, COLIN. Underdevelopment in Kenya: The Political Economy of Neo-Colonialism, 1964-71. Heinemann, London, 1975, 284 pp.
Applies the theory of underdevelopment to interpret the modern history of Kenya, especially as it concerns agriculture, foreign capital and African capitalism. Questions the view that Kenya has had a successful development experience.

02-10 MARRIS, PETER. 'Economics is not enough'. EAJ, Feb. 1967, pp. 13-18.
A review article on the Kenya government's paper on 'African Socialism and its Application to Planning in Kenya'.
See entry 02-7.

*02-11 PARKER, JAN C. 'Ideological and Economic Development in Tanzania'. African Studies Review, April 1972, pp. 43-78.

02-12 Tanzania, United Republic of. The Arusha Declaration and Tanganyika African National Union's Policy on Socialism and Self-Reliance. Tanu Publicity Section, Dar-es-Salaam, 1967, 29 pp.
A major statement of policy, defining the economic implications of Tanzania's socialist philosophy and specifying public and private enterprise areas.

02-13 Zanzibar, Government of. The Fruits of Revolution in the Islands, 1964-67. Government Printer-General, Zanzibar, 1967, 110 pp.

03 - Bibliographies; research programmes

03-1 BARNES, CAROLYN, ed. Harnessing research for production, dissemination and utilization. IDS Occasional Paper No. 5, Nairobi, 1972, 184 pp.
Proceedings of a workshop on the co-ordination of social science research.

03-2 BEDERMAN, SANFORD H. Africa: A Bibliography of Geography and Related Disciplines. Publishing Service Division, Georgia State University, 1974, 334 pp.
Includes an index of topics by country.

03-3 BOHNET, M. and REICHELT, H. Applied Research and its Impact on Economic Development: The East African Case. IFO, Munich, 1972, 210 pp.
Investigates the impact of applied research in the natural and social sciences upon economic development in East Africa.

03-4 CHANT, JOHN. Bibliography of recent farm system studies in Tanzania. Mimeographed. E.R.B., May 1968, 5 pp.
Contains references to sources on the economic characteristics of farming systems in Tanzania.

03-5 COOPER, ST. G. C. Agricultural Research in Tropical Africa. East African Literature Bureau, Nairobi, 1970, 193 pp.
Examines agronomic and economic research needed to contribute to rapid agricultural growth.

03-6 COURT, DAVID. 'An Inventory of Research on Education in Kenya'. Mimeographed. IDS Disc P 108, May 1971, 39 pp.
A bibliographic essay consisting of an annotated survey of completed and current research on education.

03-7 FRIEDLAND, WILLIAM H. Unions, Labor and Industrial Relations in Africa: An Annotated Bibliography. Center for International Studies, Cornell University, New York, 1965, 157 pp.
Covers publications in 1920 to 1965.

03-8 GARVER, R. A., ed. Research Priorities for East Africa. East African Publishing House, Nairobi, 1966, 102 pp.
Papers and recommendations on a wide range of research in East Africa.

03-9 LURY, D. A. 'National Accounts Bibliography for East Africa, 1962-64'. Mimeographed. IDS Disc P 9, 1965, 5 pp.

The Economies of East Africa

GENERAL STUDIES

(LURY, D. A.)
Lists publications on national accounts and other relevant items, using *Statistical Abstracts* and *Quarterly Economic and Statistical Review* as sources.

03-10 McLOUGHLIN, PETER F. M. *Research on Agricultural Development in East Africa*. Agricultural Development Council, New York, 1967, 112 pp.
Classifies and evaluates research on rural development in East Africa indicating areas for future research. Includes an inventory and classified bibliography.

03-11 MATHEWS, DANIEL G., ed. *Implementation and Administration of Development Activities in Africa*. Mimeographed. African Bibliographic Center, Washington, 1973, 68 pp.
Bibliography encompassing material on management resources and urban services, problems of management in rural and urban development, and effects of urban and rural development on training of executive personnel in Africa.

03-12 _____. *Income and Employment Generation in Africa*. Mimeographed. African Bibliographic Center, Washington, 1973, 73 pp.
A bibliography.

03-13 _____. *Economic Cooperation and Regional Integration in Africa*. Mimeographed. African Bibliographic Center, Washington, 1973, 49 pp.
Bibliography focusing on cooperation for development.

*03-14 MEZGER, D. and LITTICH, E. *Recent English Economic Research in East Africa - a Selected Bibliography*. Mimeographed. IFO, Munich, 1967, 383 pp.

03-15 MOLNOS, ANGELA. *Development in Africa: Planning and Implementation: A Bibliography (1946-69) and Outline, with some Emphasis on Kenya, Tanzania and Uganda*. Mimeographed. East African Academy Research Information Centre, Nairobi, April 1970, 120 pp.
The outline argues that colonial plans were administrative papers but development plans in Africa are weapons to fight poverty, disease, ignorance, and instruments to achieve economic independence.

03-16 OBUDHO, R. A. *Urbanization, City and Regional Planning of Metropolitan Kisumu, Kenya: Bibliographical Survey of an East African City*. Council of Planning Librarians, Illinois, April 1972, 26 pp.

(OBUDHO, R. A.)
A guide to literature on urbanization, city and regional planning of metropolitan Kisumu and Kenya.

03-17 OWEN, D. F., ed. Research and Development in East Africa. East African Publishing House, Nairobi, 1966, 108 pp.
Covers research topics essential to the development of East Africa.

*03-18 VON PISCHKE, J. D. Bibliography of Agricultural Credit in Kenya. IDS, Nairobi, June 1973, 19 pp.

03-19 WACHTEL, A. et al. Bibliography of Urbanisation in Kenya. Mimeographed. IDS, Nairobi, 1974, 35 pp.

03-20 WEBSTER, JOHN B. et al. A Bibliography on Kenya. Eastern African Studies Program, Syracuse University, New York, March 1967, 461 pp.
An attempt to arrange non-official publications as a base for research and library development.

1 - ECONOMIC DEVELOPMENT, PLANNING AND STABILISATION

10 - Growth and development: measurement and experiences

10-1 ALLEN, C. and KING, K. J., eds. Developmental trends in Kenya. Centre of African Studies, Edinburgh University, 1972, 337 pp.
A collection of papers on various aspects of development.

10-2 CHERNIAVSKY, MARK. Development prospects in East Africa: Kenya, Tanzania and Uganda. Chr. Michelsen Institute, Bergen, November 1965, 112 pp.
Presents a statistical analysis of structural change in the East African economy, with projections to 1985.

10-3 East African Statistical Department. 'An Index of Economic Activity for East Africa'. Econ Stat Rev, March 1963, pp. VIII - XVI.
Estimates an index of economic activity and its relationship to other economic aggregates.

10-4 EHRLICH, CYRIL. 'Some Aspects of Economic Policy in Tanganyika, 1945-1960'. J Mod Afr Studs, July 1964, pp. 265-277.

THE ECONOMIES OF EAST AFRICA

GENERAL STUDIES

(EHRLICH, CYRIL)
Shows how trade and aid were insufficient to transform the Tanganyikan economy before independence.

10-5 HELLEINER, G. K. 'The measurement of aggregative economic performance in East Africa'. EAER, July 1968, No. 1, pp. 87-93.
Discusses the adjustment of national accounts for the effect of changing prices, with special attention to terms of trade effects.

10-6 Kenya, Central Bureau of Statistics. The Growth of the Economy, 1954-1962. Government Printer, Nairobi, 1963, 18 pp.
An analysis based on national accounting, employment and trade data.

10-7 KHAMIS, I. A. 'Zanzibar's Economic Revolution'. EAJ, Feb. 1972, pp. 19-25.
Briefly discusses the social, economic and political causes of the 1964 revolution and post-revolution developments.

10-8 NYERERE, JULIUS K. 'Tanzania, ten years after independence'. African Review, June 1972, pp. 1-54.
A general review of progress in each major sector of the economy.

10-9 OLOYA, J. J. Some Aspects of Economic Development, With Special Reference to East Africa. East African Literature Bureau, Nairobi, 1968, 151 pp.
Covers problems of price fluctuations, marketing, agricultural efficiency, and the role of agriculture and industrialization in economic development.

10-10 ROBINSON, E. A. G., ed. Economic Development for Africa South of the Sahara. MacMillan, London, 1963, 744 pp.
Includes: D. Walker, "Problems of Economic Development of East Africa". Examines the main characteristics of the economies of East Africa, the processes of economic development and some lessons from experience.

10-11 RWEYEMAMU, A. H., ed. Nation-building in Tanzania. East African Publishing House, Nairobi, 1970, 109 pp.
Collection of papers providing background facts and analysing plans and performance of key sectors of the economy.

10-12 Uganda, Ministry of Planning and Community Development, Statistics Division. The Real Growth of the Economy of Uganda, 1954-1962. Government Printer, Entebbe, 1964, 50 pp.

11 - General development strategies and policies

11-1 CLIFFE, LIONEL and SAUL, JOHN S., eds. Socialism in Tanzania; Vol. 2: Policies. East African Publishing House, Nairobi, 1972.
A collection of papers which focus on development strategies underlying policy-making from the first five-year plan through the Arusha Declaration period to the second five-year plan.

11-2 HELMSCHROTT, H. Development and Development Policy in East Africa: Kenya. IFO, Munich, 1965, 133 pp.
Assesses development planning, multilateral and bilateral assistance, and suggests ways of improving the utlisation of existing resources.

11-3 KHAKEE, ABDUL. Development and Planning in Tanzania. Studentlitteratur, Lund, 1970, 123 pp.
A guide to development policies in Tanzania since independence, with a discussion of implementation problems.

11-4 MALIMA, K. A. 'International trade and economic transformation of Tanzania'. African Review, Sept. 1971, pp. 76-90.
Suggests that a balance between 'outward looking' and 'inward looking' strategies is necessary for national development.

11-5 NATTRASS, JILL. 'An evaluation of the Kenyan development strategy'. South African Journal of Economics, Sept. 1971, pp. 279-299.
Concludes that whilst Kenya has experienced satisfactory economic growth, the long run outlook is somewhat bleaker.

11-6 OSER, JACOB. Promoting Economic Development, with Illustrations from Kenya. East African Publishing House, Nairobi, 1967, 242 pp.
A general survey of development strategies and policies.

11-7 SCHNITTGER, L. Development and Development Policy in East Africa - Tanzania. IFO, Munich, 1965, 163 pp.
Assesses development planning, multilateral and bilateral assistance, and suggests ways of improving the utilisation of existing resources.

ECONOMIC DEVELOPMENT

11-8 SEIDMAN, ANN. Comparative Development Strategies in East Africa. East African Publishing House, Nairobi, 1972, 299 pp.
Compares the strategies of Kenya, Uganda and Tanzania in the 1960's, focusing on the different approaches to national planning and their impact on key sectors, such as industry, agriculture, trade and finance. Develops an informal model of the East African economies; considers the implications of the analysis for regional co-operation. See also articles in EAJ, May, June and August, 1970.

11-9 STEWART, FRANCES. Kenya: Strategies for Development. Mimeographed. Institute of Commonwealth Studies, Oxford, 1974, 29 pp.
A critical review of post-independence development strategy, and a pessimistic appraisal of neo-classical and 'redistribution from growth' alternatives.

12 - Development planning and implementation

12-1 CLARK, PAUL G. Development Planning in East Africa. East African Publishing House, Nairobi, 1965, 153 pp.
A comparative study of development planning, utilising a statistical projection model as a basis of assessment. See also the author's articles in EAER, June 1965 and June 1967, and J Mod Afr Studs, May 1966.

12-2 _____. 'Towards more comprehensive planning in East Africa'. EAER, Dec. 1963, pp. 65-74.
Discusses the pre-conditions for comprehensive planning, sector co-ordination, and project analysis.

12-3 EDWARDS, EDGAR O. 'Development Planning in Kenya since Independence'. EAER, Dec. 1968, pp. 1-15.
Examines the order of priorities among planning functions that govern the planning process in Kenya, and points out the usefulness of objective critics of the planning process.

12-4 FABER, MIKE and SEERS, DUDLEY, eds. The Crisis in Planning. 2 vols. Chatto and Windus, London, 1972, pp. 192, 221.
Volume 2 includes: Van Arkadie, B. 'Planning in Tanzania'; Ghai, D. 'The Machinery of Planning in Kenya'.

*12-5 General Agreement on Tariffs and Trade (Gatt). Development Plan Studies: The Uganda Development Plan, 1961-1966. Geneva, 1966, 137 pp.

12-6 GHAI, DHARAM P. 'How good is Kenya's plan?' EAJ, July 1964, pp. 19-28.
A discussion of the limitations of the 1964-70 Development Plan.

12-7 GRAY, CLIVE S. 'Development planning in East Africa: a review article'. EAER, Dec. 1966, pp. 1-18.
A critical review of Paul Clark's Development Planning in East Africa.
See entry 12-2. A reply by Clark is in EAER, June 1967.

12-8 GREEN, REGINALD H. 'Cautious growth promotion and cautious structuralism: the Kenya and Uganda 1966 Development Plans'. EAER, Dec. 1966, pp. 19-34.
Compares the two plans, drawing attention to differences in the strategies they propound and evaluating their quality as technical documents.

12-9 _____. 'Four African development plans: Ghana, Kenya, Nigeria and Tanzania'. J Mod Afr Studs, Aug. 1965, pp. 249-279.
A comparative discussion of planning processes, economic strategies and problems of plan implementation.

12-10 _____. 'Some problems of national development planning and foreign financing'. Uchumi, 1972, pp. 1-14.
Discusses budgetary and aid aspects of planning.

12-11 HELLEINER, G. K. 'Tanzania's second plan: socialism and self-reliance'. EAJ, Dec. 1968, pp. 41-50.
Suggestions for avoiding repetition of past mistakes and for making the most of scarce planning resources.

12-12 Kenya, Ministry of Finance. Development Plan, 1964-70. Government Printer, Nairobi, 1964, 137 pp.

12-13 Kenya, Ministry of Finance and Planning. Development Plan, 1966-1970. Government Printer, Nairobi, 1966, 384 pp.

12-14 _____. Development Plan 1974-1978. 2 vols. Government Printer, Nairobi, 1974, pp. 526, 198.
Part I deals with overall objectives, priorities and overall sector plans; Part II sets out public sector programmes and projects.

*12-15 Kenya, Republic of. Development Plan, 1970-74. Government Printer, Nairobi, 1969, 571 pp.

ECONOMIC DEVELOPMENT

12-16 _____. Plan Performance and Expectations, 1969-74, Part I. Government Printer, Nairobi, April 1972, 77 pp.
Presents a review of the performance of the plan up to 1972 and indicates additional external financing required to attain remaining plan targets.

12-17 LEYS, COLIN et al. EAJ (special issue on Kenya's Second Development Plan), March 1970, pp. 4-49.
Includes: Leys, 'Political and administrative aspects of the Plan'; Rado, Emil, 'Employment, incomes policy: Kenya's new development plan'; Mitchell, Frank, 'Macro aspects of the plan'; Hopcraft, Peter M., 'Some notes on the industrial development aspects of the plan'; Smith, L. D., 'Agriculture and rural development in Kenya'.

12-18 LIVINGSTONE, IAN. Socialist Planning in Tanzania: The Second Five Years. ERB, 1969, 29 pp.
Attempts to bring out the main features of the second five-year plan, and proceeds to a more general discussion of development planning with special reference to Tanzania.

12-19 NNOLI, OKWUDIBA. 'External stimuli and national planning in Tanzania'. The African Review, Jan. 1972, pp. 8-28.
Examines the 1961-64 and 1964-69 plans and concludes that foreign advisers and the external environment make a major impact on the content of national planning.

12-20 PACKARD, PHILIP C. and WIT, DANIEL. 'Government and the implementation of economic plans in new and emerging states: an addendum'. Development and Change, 1972-73, No. 3, pp. 1-11.
Use planning experience in Tanzania to argue that project planning can be an effective alternative to comprehensive planning.

12-21 RWEYEMAMU, A. H. Managing Planned Development: Tanzania's Experience. Mimeographed. East African Institute of Social Research, Conference Proceedings, Part B, Jan. 1966, 18 pp.
Plan implementation depends on the type of bureaucracy and degree of commitment of the political leadership.

12-22 SAUL, JOHN S. 'Planning for socialism in Tanzania: the socio-political context'. Development and Change, 1971-72, No. 3, pp. 3-25.
Criticises the treatment of development planning as a technical and organisational matter, and argues that planning for socialist development is first and foremost an ideological and political question.

12-23 Tanzania, Ministry of Economic Affairs and Development Planning. First Year Progress Report on the Implementation of the Five-year Development Plan; Public Sector; July 1964 to June 1965. Government Printer, Dar-es-Salaam, 1965, 16 pp.

12-24 Tanzania, United Republic of. Second Five-year Plan for Economic and Social Development, July 1969 to June 1974. 4 vols. Government Printer, Dar-es-Salaam, 1969, pp. 227, 115, 327, 18.
Vol. I: General analysis; Vol. II: The programme; Vol. III: Regional perspectives; Vol. IV: Survey of the high and middle level manpower requirements and resources.

12-25 _____. Tanganyika Five-year Plan for Economic and Social Development, July, 1964-June, 1969. 2 vols. Government Printer, Dar-es-Salaam, 1964, pp. 114; 151.
Vol. I: A general analysis outlining the development programmes of public sector and investments expected from private sector; Vol. II: A detailed description of development programmes to be financed through the central Government.

12-26 Uchumi Editorial Board. Towards Socialist Planning. Tanzania Publishing House, Dar-es-Salaam, 1972, 199 pp.
Collected essays on Tanzania's socialist planning, on the theme that planning should not be a mere technocratic exercise but must also involve the people and the Party.

*12-27 Uganda, Ministry of Finance, Planning and Economic Development. Third Five-year Development Plan, 1971/72-1975/76. Government Printer, Entebbe, 1972, 428 pp.

*12-28 Uganda, Ministry of Planning. The First Five-year Development Plan, 1961/62-1965/66: Progress Report. Government Printer, Entebbe, 1966, 33 pp.

*12-29 Uganda, Ministry of Planning and Economic Development. Work for Progress: Uganda's Second Five-year Plan 1966-71 and Supplement of Projects. 2 vols. Government Printer, Kampala, 1969, pp. 182, 268.

*12-30 Uganda, Republic of. The First Five-year Development Plan, 1961/62 to 1965/66. Government Printer, Kampala, 1963, 113 pp.

12-31 VENTE, ROLF E. Planning Process: The East African Case. Weltforum Verlag, Munich, 1970, 233 pp.

ECONOMIC DEVELOPMENT

(VENTE, ROLF E.)
Criticises past, conventional, approaches to planning and urges a new approach in which planning is used continuously as a device for preparing decisions.

13 - Macro-economic models

13-1 BLACK, DAVID E. 'An employment and output projection model for Kenya and Nairobi'. Mimeographed. IDS Disc P 172, June 1973, 29 pp.
Reports on a simulation model designed to predict employment and output for Kenya and Nairobi. Tests employment implications of future changes, e.g. due to population growth.

13-2 DAHL, H. E. and FAALAND, J. The Economy of Tanzania. Christian Michelsen Institute, Bergen, Aug. 1967, 131 pp.
Econometric study of structural relationships, 1956-1965, with projections of trade and resource for 1970 and 1975.

13-3 FAALAND, J. and DAHL, H. E. The Economy of Kenya. Christian Michelsen Institute, Bergen, July 1967, 141 pp.
Econometric study of structural relationships, 1956-1965, with projections of trade and resource gaps for 1970 and 1975.

13-4 _____. The Economy of Uganda. Christian Michelsen Institute, Bergen, Sept. 1967, 134 pp.
Econometric study of structural relationships, 1956-1965, with projections of trade and resource gaps for 1970 and 1975.

13-5 HOWE, CHARLES W. and KARANI, HIRAM. 'A projection model for the Kenya economy: A study in development planning and comparative economic structures'. EAER, June 1965, pp. 21-31.
Use an econometric representation to compare the structure of the Kenyan economy with those of Tanzania and Uganda, and to analyse the implications of Kenya's 1964-70 Development Plan.
See also note by Massell in EAER, June 1967.

13-6 IRERI, D. 'A proposed model to analyse economic interdependence among the member countries of the East African Community'. EAER, Dec. 1969, pp. 75-87.

(IRERI, D.)
Points to the importance of the construction of a modified input-output model and suggests that this will enable consistency in the disaggregation of important sectors.

13-7 KARANI, H. 'A projection model for the Kenya economy: implications of the Kenya Development Plan, 1966-1970'. EAER, June 1967, pp. 45-54.
Presents a simple econometric model of the Kenya economy and analyses its implications for the Plan.

13-8 TOBIN, JAMES. 'Estimates of Sectoral Capital/Output'. IDS Disc P 171, 1973, 12 pp.
Calculates alternative capital/output ratios for fourteen sectors of the Kenyan economy and discusses the capital costs of providing jobs.

13-9 VAN ARKADIE, BRIAN. Nature of Structural Analysis of East African Economies. Mimeographed. East African Institute of Social Research, Conference Proceedings, Jan. 1965, 35 pp.
Uses a macro-economic approach to analyse the relation between major sectors and the behaviour of aggregate variables in East Africa since 1945.

13-10 _____. The Structure of the Kenya Economy. Mimeographed. East African Institute of Social Research, Conference Proceedings, Part C, Jan. 1964, 5 pp.
An exercise in applied macro-economics which attempts to produce a synoptic view of the economy based on existing sectoral data.

14 - Public and development administration

14-1 BROKENSHA, DAVID and NELLIS, JOHN. 'Administration in Kenya, a study of Mbere'. 2 parts. J Admin Overseas, Oct. 1974 and Jan. 1975, pp. 510-23, pp. 17-29.
Part I examines the role of provincial administration, the district officer, the chief and the sub-chief; Part II studies departmental endeavours in Mbere, particularly agricultural and ancillary staff to see how far the administration is really developmental when confronted with conflict between tradition and innovation.

14-2 CHEGE, MICHAEL. 'Systems management and the plan implementation process in Kenya'. Mimeographed. IDS Disc P 179, Nov. 1972, 22 pp.

ECONOMIC DEVELOPMENT

(CHEGE, MICHAEL)
The ubiquity of uncertainty is seen as militating against the introduction of systems procedures and as necessitating unprogrammed, ad hoc and flexible administrative techniques.

14-3 COLLINS, P. 'The working of Tanzania's Rural Development Fund: a problem in decentralisation'. EAJ Rural Devel, 1972, Nos. 1 and 2, pp. 141-162.
Discusses the conditions necessary to make the Fund successful in village development schemes.

14-4 CONYERS, DIANA. 'Organisation for development--the Tanzanian experience'. J Admin Overseas, July 1974, pp. 438-49.
Discusses the dissolution of a traditional centralised ministerial structure and the establishment of development authorities at regional and local levels.

14-5 DRYDEN, STANLEY. Local Administration in Tanzania. East African Publishing House, Nairobi, 1968, 178 pp.
Shows steps by which the Tanzanian authorities changed the English institutions they inherited into more flexible instruments, adjusted to the tasks of rural development.

*14-6 FULLER, C. and CHAMBERS, R. 'Training for the administration of development in Kenya'. J Admin Overseas, April 1965.

*14-7 HUNTER, GUY. 'Development administration in East Africa'. J Admin Overseas, 1967.

14-8 HYDEN, GORAN. 'Social structure, bureaucracy and development administration in Kenya'. African Review, Jan. 1972, pp. 118-129.
Expresses doubts about the possibility of transforming the Kenyan civil service into a 'development administration' without a series of accompanying measures.

14-9 HYDEN, GORAN; JACKSON, ROBERT; and OKUMU, JOHN, eds. Development Administration: The Kenyan Experience. Oxford University Press, Nairobi, 1970, 366 pp.
A collection of essays on the theme of how public administration relates and addresses itself to development problems in Kenya. Includes contributions on the political and economic environment, aid, rural development, trade unions, and co-operatives.

14-10 KEEGAN, WARREN J. Case Studies in the Management of Economic Development. Oxford University Press, Nairobi, 1968, 68 pp.

(KEEGAN, WARREN J.)
Discusses cases and problems in public administration in East Africa.

14-11 Kenya, Republic of. Report of the Commission of Inquiry (Public Service Structure and Remuneration Commission). D. N. Ndegwa, Chairman. Government Printer, Nairobi, May 1971, 397 pp.
Investigates matters affecting organisation and structure, recruitment and remuneration in Kenya's public service, and makes recommendations.

14-12 _____. Report of the Committee of Review into the Kenya Institute of Administration. Adu, A. L. Chairman. Government Printer, Nairobi, 1965, 68 pp.
Studies the existing programmes and organisation, the role of the Institute, and advises on future programmes.

14-13 LEONARD, D. K., ed. Rural Administration in Kenya. East African Literature Bureau, Nairobi, 1973, 165 pp.
Collection of essays presenting analyses of administration in rural Kenya, with proposals for improving its quality, especially in economic planning and agricultural development.

14-14 PRATT, R. CRANFORD. 'The administration of economic planning in a newly independent state: the Tanzanian experience, 1963-1966'. Journal of Commonwealth Political Studies, 1967, pp. 38-59.

14-15 RWEYEMAMU, ANTHONY H. and HYDEN, GORAN, eds. A Decade of Public Administration in Africa. East African Literature Bureau, Nairobi, 1975, 377 pp.
Reproduces the views of African public servants as presented to a series of inter-African public administration seminars. Includes papers on professionalisation, reform, delegation to public enterprise, and decision-making. Presents Tanzanian and Kenyan materials.

14-16 SPERBER, K. W. Public Administration in Tanzania. Weltforum Verlag, Munich, 1970, 120 pp.
Compares German and British administrative systems and discusses their influence on modern administration in Tanzania.

14-17 TORDOFF, WILLIAM. 'Regional administration in Tanzania'. J Mod Afr Studs, May 1965, pp. 63-89.

(TORDOFF, WILLIAM)
Reviews the role of the Tanzania African National Union, the local control vested in regional commissioners, and their contributions to development.

14-18 TRAPMAN, CHRISTOPHER. Change in Administrative Structures: A Case Study of Kenyan Agricultural Development. Overseas Development Institute, London, 1974, 100 pp.
Examines how well the present machinery serving the agricultural sector has adapted to small-scale farmers, and its sensitivity to the needs of the agricultural sector.

15 - Domestic economic fluctuations and forecasting; inflation

15-1 KIMBLE, HELEN. Price Control in Tanzania. Economic Research Bureau, Dar-es-Salaam, 1970, 55 pp.
Surveys the advantages and limitations of price control as an instrument of government policy.

15-2 KIMBLE, H. and ANDERSON, O. M. The control of retail prices in Tanzania. National Price Control Advisory Board, Dar-es-Salaam, Dec. 1967, 63 pp.
Argues in favour of price controls to protect consumers, reduce profits and guard against inflation.

16 - Consumption and saving studies

16-1 BINHAMMER, H. H. The Institutional Framework for Mobilizing Savings in Tanzania. ERB, 1969, 17 pp.
Argues that higher incomes are necessary if saving is to be increased, and examines how self-help investment projects and extension services could increase real saving.

16-2 CLEAVE, J. H. 'Food consumption in Uganda'. EAJ Rural Devel, Jan. 1968, pp. 70-87.
Attempts to assess food requirements in Uganda and compares it with an estimate of food availability in 1963.

16-3 East African Statistical Department. The Patterns of Income, Expenditure and Consumption of Unskilled Workers in Zanzibar: Report on a Survey Carried out in April 1962. Nairobi, 1963, 25 pp.

16-4 HOWE, C. W. 'An analysis of African household consumption and financial behaviour in Kenya and Uganda'. EAER, June 1968, pp. 51-61.

(HOWE, C. W.)
An attempt to estimate Engel Curves and to explain expenditure behaviour of various income groups.

16-5 _____. 'The use of sample household surveys in economic planning with some empirical results for East Africa'. OEIS Bull, 1966, pp. 199-209.
Stresses the value of household surveys covering the major consumer groups (racial, tribal, geographical) which can be expected to exhibit different patterns of expenditure relative to income.

16-6 Kenya, Central Bureau of Statistics. 'Estimates of the income elasticity of demand for various items in Nairobi, Mombasa and Kisumu'. K. Stat Dig, June 1972, pp. 1-8.
A study based on the 1969 household budget survey.

16-7 _____. 'Middle Income Index of Consumer Prices, Nairobi' K. Stat Dig, Dec. 1964, pp. 1-3.
Presents a consumer price index based on the consumption patterns of African households in Nairobi with an annual income of 200 to 750.

16-8 _____. New Lower and Middle Income Cost of Living Indices, 1971. Nairobi, 1971, 16 pp.
A description of methods of compilation, based on a 1969 household budget survey.

16-9 _____. The Pattern of Income, Expenditure and Consumption of African Middle Income Workers in Nairobi. Government Printer, Nairobi, July 1964, 52 pp.
Surveys the spending habits of households in Nairobi having an income of £200 to £750 p.a., using households as the unit of analysis.
See also summary in K. Stat Dig, June 1964.

16-10 MASSELL, BENTON F. 'Determinants of household expenditure in rural Kenya'. IDS Disc P 49, April 1967, 39 pp.
Based on budget study data of Central Province; provides a better understanding of how households in rural areas spend their income in relation to household size and other social and economic variables.

16-11 MASSEL, BENTON F. and HEYER, JUDITH. 'Householder expenditure in Nairobi: a statistical analysis of consumer behaviour'. Econ Dev Cult Change, Jan. 1969, pp. 212-234.
Presents the methods adopted and estimates expenditure elasticities for 26 groups of goods and services from a sample of 300 middle-income African households in Nairobi.

FISCAL AND FINANCIAL TOPICS

16-12 MASSEL, B. F. and PARNES, A. 'Estimation of expenditure elasticities from a sample of rural households in Uganda'. OIES Bull, 1969, No. 4, pp. 313-29.
Employs two-stage least squares analysis to estimate expenditure functions in the Fort Portal area.

16-13 SNOWDEN, P. N. 'Preliminary report on a study of company savings in Kenya's manufacturing sector'. Mimeographed. IDS Disc P 113, Aug. 1971, 16 pp.
Examines the nature and magnitude of company internally generated funds as a source of finance for economic development.

16-14 Tanzania, Bureau of Statistics. Family Budget Survey of Middle-grade African Civil Servants, 1963. Government Printer, Dar-es-Salaam, 1964, 52 pp.
Presents budget data for urban African families earning £400 to £1,000 p.a., analysed by demographic and social background.

16-15 ______. 1969 Household Budget Survey. 3 vols. Government Printer, Dar-es-Salaam, 1972, pp. 221; 82; 90.
Results of the first country-wide household survey, describing methods and including data on income, consumption, prices and housing conditions, by region.

16-16 Uganda, Statistics Department. Patterns of Income, Expenditure and Consumption of African Unskilled Workers, Kampala 1964, Jinja 1965. Kampala, 1965 and 1966.

2 - FISCAL AND FINANCIAL TOPICS

20 - Public finance and budgeting

20-1 CLARKE, J. R. 'East Africa: estimation of import duties on transferred goods'. Mimeographed. IDS Disc P 45, Feb. 1967, 7 pp.
Divides these imports into two groups: 'reference goods' and 'broken bulk' goods, defining their meaning. Recommends the use of a 'proportion transferred' method for its conceptual simplicity.

20-2 DAVEY, K. J., ed. Programme Budgeting for East Africa. East African Staff College, Nairobi, 1972, 130 pp.
A handbook including an illustrative application to educational budgeting in Uganda.

20-3 DAVID, WILFRED L., ed. Public Finance, Planning and Economic Development. MacMillan, London, 1973, 349 pp.
Includes: Jetha, Nizar, 'Some aspects of domestic financing of central government expenditure: the case of Kenya'.

20-4 DIEJOMAOH, VICTOR. 'Financing local government authorities in Kenya'. Mimeographed. IDS Disc P 96, Sept. 1970. 42 pp.
Investigates the determinants and adequacy of local government revenue sources; suggests ways of increasing revenues.

20-5 _____. 'Taxation and government savings in Kenya'. EAER, Dec. 1970, pp. 15-30.
Argues that the contribution of government savings to the finance of development is relatively low, and hence an attempt should be made to increase government savings by increasing the growth of tax revenue.

20-6 DUE, J. F. 'The Uganda sales tax on importation and manufacture'. EAER, June 1969, pp. 1-16.
Suggests that the Uganda tax is productive of revenue, feasible of effective administration and not disruptive of economic development.

20-7 ENGLAND, J. O. 'Graduated personal tax in Kenya'. J Admin Overseas, Oct. 1964, pp. 204-13.
Explores the possibilities of establishing a pay-as-you can arrangement.

20-8 GHAI, DHARAM P. Taxation for Development: A Case Study of Uganda. East African Publishing House, Nairobi, 1966, 132 pp.
Employs an income elasticity criterion to evaluate Uganda's tax structure and to make suggestions for improvement.

20-9 HELLER, PETER S. 'Public investment in LDC's with recurrent cost constraint: the Kenyan case'. Quarterly Journal of Economics, May 1974, pp. 251-76.
Analyses the role of inter-temporal public sector budgetary constraints in limiting the size and composition of present public investment expenditures that can be utilised productively, using Kenyan plan and fiscal data.

20-10 HICKS, U. K. 'The revenue implications of the Uganda and Tanzania Plans'. J Dev Studs, April 1966, pp. 234-253.
Discusses the future growth and development of the two economies and their resulting fiscal needs.

FISCAL AND FINANCIAL TOPICS

20-11 KENT, A. W. Report of the Services to be Administered by Local Authorities in Tanganyika and the Consequential Financial Arrangements. Government Printer, Dar-es-Salaam, 1963.

20-12 Kenya, Republic of. Fiscal Commission Report, 1963. R. C. Tress, Chairman. Government Printer, Nairobi, 1963, 125 pp. Examines the fiscal structure and its revenue potential, with recommendations.

20-13 LEE, EUGENE C. Local Taxation in Tanzania. Oxford University Press, London, 1965, 66 pp.
Discusses the structure of, and alternatives for, taxation at the local level.

20-14 LURY, D. A. and SHAH, H. H. 'Local government in Kenya: income and expenditure, 1959-1961'. EAER, June 1966, pp. 69-86.
A survey of sources and allocation of local government finances.

20-15 MITCHELL, FRANK. 'Forecasts of returns to Kajiado County Council from the Masai Amboseli Game Reserve, 1970-2000'. Mimeographed. IDS Disc P 87, Nov. 1969, 12 pp.
Studies the determinants of the future value of revenue from this source and forecasts revenue on the basis of alternative policy assumptions.

20-16 NELLIS, J. R. 'Who pays taxes in Kenya?' The African Review, 1972, No. 2, pp. 345-364.
Concludes that the tax system is regressive and there is much income tax evasion.

20-17 NYANGIRA, NICHOLAS. Relative Modernisation and Public Resource Allocation in Kenya. East African Literature Bureau, Nairobi, 1975, 169 pp.
Examines allocations of public resources to agriculture, commerce, education and self-help projects. Contends that variations in the level of modernisation determine resource allocations to regions, districts and villages.

20-18 PENNER, R. G. Financing Local Government in Tanzania. East African Publishing House, Nairobi, 1970, 102 pp.
Discusses limitations that the relative poverty of Tanzanian local government places on its role in economic development.

20-19 ROZENTAL, ALEK A. 'Metropolitan revenue sources: the Nairobi case'. IDS Disc P 191, Dec. 1973, 13 pp.
Using Nairobi case materials, discusses reasons for the budgetary plight of large cities in developing countries. Suggests a substitute tax measure to replace the abolished graduated personal tax in Nairobi and improve the city's revenue structure.

20-20 SEELY, H. C. 'Local government development finance (Kenya)'. J Admin Overseas, Oct. 1964, pp. 191-203.

20-21 TAYLOR, MILTON C., ed. Taxation for African Economic Development. African Publishing Corporation, New York, 1969, 556 pp.
Includes: Nizar, Jetha 'Company taxation in East Africa'; Due, J. F. and Robson, P. 'Tax harmonization in the East African Common Market'.

20-22 Uganda, Republic of. Tax Enquiry Report 1964/65. F. Vallibhay, Chairman. Government Printer, Kampala, 1965, 208 pp.
An evaluation of Uganda's tax system. Special emphasis on the income tax and graduated tax, and on the repercussions of the East African Common Market.

20-23 U. N. Economic Commission for Africa. 'Some aspects of public finance and industrial development in East Africa'. Econ Bull Afr, 1968, pp. 11-34.
Explores the inter-relationships between public finance and industrial development.

20-24 WESTLAKE, M. J. 'Tax evasion, tax incidence and the distribution of income in Kenya'. EAER, Dec. 1973, pp. 1-27.
Concludes that the incidence of the structure of personal income taxes and indirect taxes on the distribution of income is slightly regressive; evasion of the graduated personal tax was less than of the income tax; evasion of both tends to strengthen the regressive nature of the structure.

21 - Domestic financial institutions and markets; money and credit

21-1 AROWOLO, EDWARD A. 'The development of capital markets in Africa, with particular reference to Kenya and Nigeria'. IMF Staff Papers, July 1971, pp. 420-469.
Includes an examination of attempts to establish an organised capital market in Kenya.

FISCAL AND FINANCIAL TOPICS

21-2 BINHAMMER, H. H. Institutional Arrangements for Supplying Credit and Finance to the Rural Sector of the Economy in Tanzania. ERB, 1968, 28 pp.
Studies the National Co-operative Development Bank to compare the financial transactions of the rural sector with the country's overall plan.

21-3 BOSA, GEORGE R. The Financing of Small-Scale Enterprises in Uganda. Oxford University Press, Nairobi, 1969, 105 pp.
Examines the sources of funds available to small enterprises, and the problems and difficulties they encounter.

21-4 CASELLI, CLARA. The Banking System of Tanzania. Cassa Di Risparnio Delle, Milan, 1975, 350 pp.
Outlines the development of the credit system in East Africa. Describes Tanzania's banking and credit system, discussing problems of monetary and credit policy.

21-5 CHANT, JOHN F. Some Problems of Agricultural Credit in Tanzania. Mimeographed. East African Institute of Social Research Conference Proceedings, Kampala, Jan. 1968, 22 pp.
Describes existing agricultural credit extension and suggests well managed credit agencies to ensure continued availability of funds.

21-6 ENGBERG, H. L. 'Commercial banking in East Africa, 1950-1963'. J Mod Afr Studs, Aug. 1965, pp. 175-200.
Discusses why banks lag behind political, social and economic changes, and the functions of the financial system.

21-7 GERSHENBERG, IRVING. 'Banking in Uganda since Independence'. Econ Dev Cult Change, April 1972, pp. 504-523.
An analysis of the commercial banking system.

21-8 _____. Commercial Banking in Uganda: Prescriptions for Economic Development. Makerere Institute of Social Research, Kampala, Aug. 1973, 61 pp.
Analyses commercial banking since independence and suggests policies to enhance its contribution to economic development.

21-9 _____. 'Multinationals and development: Commercial banking in Uganda'. Africa Today, 1973, No. 4, pp. 19-27.
Concludes that British colonial banking was geared to maintaining the flow of raw material exports to the developed countries; criticises their training programmes.

21-10 HUNT, DIANA. Credit for Agricultural Development: A Case Study of Uganda. East African Publishing House, Nairobi, 1975, 400 pp.

Focuses on uses made, and impact of, loans; also assesses the Progressive Farmers' Loan and Co-operative Credit Schemes.

See also articles in EAJ Rural Devel 1972, Nos. 1 and 2, and 1974.

21-11 International Bank for Reconstruction and Development. A Survey of Farm Credit in Kenya. Mimeographed. G. F. Donaldson, and J. D. von Pischke, Consultants. International Development Association, Washington, 1973. 207 pp.

Part I reviews credit provisions and requirements in the farm sector. Part II details the major institutions and programmes providing farm credit.

21-12 JELLICOE, M. R. Indigenous Savings Associations in Eastern Africa and Mobilisation of Domestic Savings. U. N. Economic Commission for Africa, Addis Ababa, 1968, 71 pp.

21-13 JORGENSEN, N. O. The Case for Cooperative Loan Associations in Kenya. Mimeographed. East African Institute of Social Research, Conference Proceedings, Part A, Jan. 1966, 22 pp.

Discusses the need for credit, and actual co-operative financing of small-scale enterprises.

21-14 _____. 'I.C.D.C. (Industrial and Commercial Development Corporation): its purpose and performance'. IDS Disc P 47, April 1967, 19 pp.

Discusses problems involved in public lending to private small-scale enterprises, and suggests solutions.

21-15 Kenya, Central Bank of. Money and Banking in Kenya. Nairobi, ca. 1973, 34 pp.

A descriptive survey of monetary and capital institutions, and their regulation.

21-16 KRATZ, JOACHIM W. 'The East African Currency Board'. International Monetary Fund, Staff Papers, 1966, pp. 229-253.

21-17 LOXLEY, J. 'Building society instability in Kenya'. Mimeographed. IDS Disc P 8, Feb. 1965, 16 pp.

Aims at discovering the causes of a crisis that occurred among building societies in Kenya and how this disaster was averted. Examines future prospects in the light of past experience.

FISCAL AND FINANCIAL TOPICS

21-18 LOXLEY, J. Financial Intermediaries and their Role in East Africa. Mimeographed. Makerere Institute of Social Research, Conference Papers, Jan. 1967, 27 pp.
Examines financial institutions' impact upon savings, investment, balance of payments and money supply, with emphasis on non-bank institutions.

21-19 _____. 'Financial planning and control in Tanzania'. Development and Change, 1971-72, No. 3, pp. 43-61.
Traces the major institutional changes in Tazania's monetary and financial system since independence; concludes by examining the present state of financial planning and its defects.

21-20 LOYNES, J. B. From Currency Board to Central Bank. Economics Club of Kenya, May 1963, 10 pp.
Reviews monetary developments in East Africa, 1960-63, and draws upon the experiences of other recently-independent countries in establishing their monetary systems.

21-21 MARRIS, PETER. 'Lending money'. J Mod Afr Studs, 1967, No. 2, pp. 163-79.
Thoughts on the role of credit in financing small-scale African enterprises and as a service African businessmen provide for their customers.

*21-22 MEAD, DONALD C. 'Monetary analysis in an underdeveloped economy: a case study of three East African territories (Kenya, Uganda and Tanganyika)'. Yale Economic Essays, Spring 1963, pp. 57-103.

21-23 NEWLYN, W. T. Finance for Development: A Study of Sources of Finance in Uganda, with Particular Reference to Credit Creation. East African Publishing House, Nairobi, 1968, 107 pp.
There is need for improved financial statistics, financial and physical planning, and credit creation to facilitate growth in income.

21-24 _____. Money in an African Context. Oxford University Press, Nairobi, 1967, 156 pp.
Uses monetary theory to analyse the development of money and banking in East Africa.

*21-25 _____. 'Statistical analysis of integration in the East African banking system'. Econ Stat Rev, Dec. 1966, pp. VIII-XII.

21-26 NSEKELA, A. J. 'The role of commercial banking in building a socialist Tanzania'. The African Review, 1974, No. 1, pp. 25-42.
Concludes that the National Bank of Commerce will have to adjust to changing circumstances in order to improve its contribution to economic development.

21-27 OKAI, M. 'The contribution of farm credit to agricultural development in Uganda'. Uganda Agricultural Society Journal, 1969, No. 1, pp. 46-55.

21-28 PAUW, E. J. Banking in East Africa. IFO, Munich, 1969, 278 pp.
Analyses the structure and development of banking in East Africa.

21-29 ROBSON, P. 'Finance, development and investment; some aspects of Kenya's problems'. EAER, June 1963, pp. 1-12.
Discusses financial requirements for development, possible means of improving the supply of investible funds, and the rate of capital formation.

21-30 SELLEKAERTS, WILLY, ed. Economic Development and Planning. Macmillan, London, 1974, 260 pp.
Includes, Letiche, John, 'Dependent Monetary Systems and Economic Development: The Case of Sterling East Africa'.

21-31 SELSJORD, MIKAEL. 'Recent developments in commercial banking in East Africa: A statistical analysis'. Econ Stat Rev, Sept. 1966, pp. VIII-XXII.
Discusses the structural features of banking, and developments in commercial banking up to 1966.

21-32 VASTHOFF, JOSEF. Small Farm Credit and Development: Some Experiences in East Africa, with Special Reference to Kenya. Weltforum Verlag, Munich, 1968, 144 pp.
Surveys financial requirements of small farms, sources of credit, and reports on a field study of the impact of smallholder credit on farm productivity.

21-33 VON PISCHKE, J. D. Credit Use and Development on Nineteen Murang'a Farms. Mimeographed. IDS Miscellaneous Paper 74d, Jan. 1974, 274 pp.
Survey carried out on a sample of small farms, focussing on the financial evidence of development impact seen in farm cash flows between 1969 and 1973.

FISCAL AND FINANCIAL TOPICS

21-34 VON PISCHKE, J. D. Farm Credit in Kenya: The Poor Farmer Paradox. Mimeographed. IDS Miscellaneous Paper 74c, Sept. 1973, 75 pp.
Discusses policies and institutional behaviour which influence the availability of formal sector credit to small-scale agriculture and attempts to develop a non-quantitative model to describe the operation of the credit delivery system.

21-35 _____. A Survey of Major Agricultural Credit Programmes and Institutions Operating in Kenya. Mimeographed. IDS Miscellaneous Paper 74B, Nov. 1973, 199 pp.
Discusses land transfers and settlement schemes since the early 1960's; operation of Agricultural Finance Corporation; short-term credit including commercial bank lending to agriculture; and experimental smallholder seasonal credit projects.

21-36 WHITE, B. S. and DOWNING, C. M. 'Some Problems in Financing Mechanization in Small-scale Agriculture'. Mimeographed. Kenya, Ministry of Agriculture, Nairobi, 1968.

22 - Domestic fiscal, financial and monetary policies

22-1 BINHAMMER, H. H. Financing Industrial Development in Tanzania. Mimeographed. ERB Paper 69/4, 1969, 36 pp.
Argues that domestic savings should be channelled into the financial system to become a source of new capital.

22-2 BOLNICK, B. R. 'A note on the behaviour of the proximate determinants of money in Kenya'. EAER, June 1975.
Shows that the money supply is not easily controlled by the Central Bank of Kenya.

22-3 DUE, J. F. 'The reform of East African taxation (Tanganyika, Kenya and Uganda)'. EAER, Dec. 1964, pp. 57-68.
Suggests changes in tax structure and mentions some goals that taxation should achieve.

22-4 GROES, N. The Possibilities of Monetary Policy in Tanzania. Mimeographed. ERB Paper No. 66/2, 1966, 17 pp.
Discusses the Bank of Tanzania Act and the possibilities it provides for monetary policies.

22-5 HASKELL, MARK A. 'Local government finance in Uganda: Taxes, expenditures and grants-in-aid'. EAER, June 1975, pp. pp. 75-83.

(HASKELL, MARK A.)
Argues that for equitable distribution two principles should be involved: 1. direct expenditures should be allocated be each ministry on an equal per capita basis among local units; 2. grants-in-aid should be allocated in relation to population (or need).

22-6 KING, J. R. 'Financial Policy in Kenya: The Background to the Reserve Crisis of 1971'. Mimeographed. IDS Disc P 186, Nov. 1973, 45 pp.
Attempts, by tracing financial developments, to explain why foreign reserves rose in 1968-70 and then declined steeply, as largely caused by the unfortunate timing of an expansionist budget and a re-building of inventories.

22-7 LOMORO, G. Money Expansion in East African Economic Development. Mimeographed. East African Institute of Social Research, Conference Proceedings, Jan. 1965, 12 pp, VIII.
Suggests how the East African money supply could be expanded to provide development capital.

22-8 LOXLEY, J. The Behaviour of the Tanzania Money Supply, 1966-1970, and the Use of Monetary Indicators. Mimeographed. ERB Paper 71/3, 1971, 59 pp.
Examines monetary data and concludes that sectoral money flows should replace money supply, foreign reserves and credit indicators for planning purposes.

22-9 _____. The Domestic Finance of Development Projects in Tanzania. Mimeographed. ERB Paper 71/8, 1971, 37 pp.
Points out that there is duplication of functions in Tanzania's financial institutions due to their unplanned activities. A planned direction of resources into productive outlets is needed.

22-10 MARLIN, PETER, ed. Financial Aspects of Development in East Africa. Weltforum Verlag, Munich, 1970, 396 pp.
A collection of five papers discussing public finance, private saving, banking, agricultural credit and the balance of payments.

22-11 NEWLYN, W. T. The Significance of Separate Monetary Systems in East Africa. Mimeographed. East African Institute of Social Research Conference Proceedings, Part A, Jan. 1966, 11 pp.
Argues that bilateral balances of Community country currencies show that partner states are striving to "beggar their neighbours"; this is likely to undermine the common market.

INTERNATIONAL TRADE

22-12 United States Agency for International Development. Report and Recommendation on Credit for Kenya Farmers by the Tootell Mission on Agriculture Credit. Robert B. Tootell, Consultant. April 1970, 33 pp.
Draws attention to limitations of past credit schemes and recommends against a large expansion of government credit. Proposes instead measures to strengthen existing schemes and institutions.

3 - INTERNATIONAL TRADE AND PAYMENTS: EAST AFRICAN CO-OPERATION

30 - International trade and trade relations; terms of trade

30-1 East African Statistical Department. 'A review of external trade of East Africa, 1962'. Econ Stat Rev, June 1963, pp. VIII-XVI.
Quantitative analysis of trade between East Africa and the rest of the world.

30-2 FRIESEN, RONALD L. 'The determinants and implications of the demand for imports: an econometric study of Kenya'. EAER, June 1975.
Finds import volumes to be responsive to income and price changes but less so to changes in tariffs.

30-3 GOODMAN, STEPHEN H. 'Eastern and Western markets for the primary products of East Africa'. EAER, June 1967, pp. 77-83.
Concludes that the western bloc have provided more stable export markets that the communist bloc.

30-4 HAMMOND, R. C. 'Manufactured exports of the EAC partner states'. Econ Stat Rev, Sept./Dec. 1972, pp. XIX-XLIV.
Presents and comments upon time series data on export of manufactures within and outside the Community.

30-5 HAZLEWOOD, ARTHUR. 'Inter-state trade in East African manufactures, 1967-70'. Econ Stat Rev, Sept. 1971, pp. VIII-XXVIII.
A statistical analysis of industrial imbalance in East Africa and its effects on inter-territorial trade.

30-6 HELLEINER, G. K. Trade, Aid and Nation-Building in Tanzania. Mimeographed. ERB, paper 67/3, 1967, 15 pp.
Argues that trade is preferable to aid for it has minimal strings.

30-7 Kenya, Central Bureau of Statistics. 'Exports of manufactured products'. K Stat Dig, March 1974, pp. 4-16.
Data on the value of Kenya's principal manufactured exports since 1964.

30-8 MARLIN, P. V. The Impact of External Economic Relations on the Economic Development of East Africa. Mimeographed. IFO, Munich, June 1966, 110 pp.
Concludes that further growth of foreign trade is indispensable for the development of Kenya, Uganda and Tanzania.

30-9 MBILINYI, S. M. 'East African export commodities and the enlarged European Economic Community'. The African Review, 1973, No. 1, pp. 85-110.
Shows that the enlarged EEC will offer various benefits but at the cost of lost Commonwealth preferences.

30-10 RAMM-ERICSON, N. and SINGH, D. C. 'Some aspects of East Africa's trade with EEC and EFTA'. Econ Stat Rev, March 1964, pp. VIII-XXIII.
Show the value of East Africa's import and export trade with EEC and EFTA countries in 1958-1963.

30-11 RAMM-ERICSON, NILS. 'The price movements in East Africa's exports'. Econ Stat Rev, June 1964, pp. XXXVII-XLVII.
Analyses year-to-year changes in world prices of some selected commodities.

30-12 ROWE, J. W. F. The World's Coffee (A Study of Economics and Politics of the Coffee Industries of Certain Countries and of the International Problem). H.M.S.O., London, 1963, 200 pp.
Discusses the world supply and demand position; studies in detail the industries of six countries, including Kenya, Tanganyika and Uganda.

30-13 SINGH, DUSHYANT C. 'A review of East Africa's trade, 1963'. Econ Stat Rev, June 1964, pp. VIII-XXXVII.
A study of the main aspects of external and interterritorial trade in 1963.

30-14 VINNAI, VOLKER. 'Kenya's external trade, 1964-1971'. Mimeographed. IDS Disc P 165, April 1973, 34 pp.
Analyses Kenya's export pattern, 1964-71, and its geographical distribution. In 1971 Kenya still relied on two agricultural cash crops, but the structure of imports was changing in favour of capital goods and away from consumer goods.

INTERNATIONAL TRADE

31 - Commercial policies

31-1 DIAMOND, P. A. 'Effective protection of the East African transfer taxes'. EAER, Dec. 1968, pp. 37-48.
Argues that for some value of tax rates and import contents Kenyan and Ugandan firms are at a disadvantage in the Tanzanian market relative to firms outside East Africa.

31-2 GHAI, DHARAM P. 'The association agreement between the European Economic Community and the partner states of the East African Community'. J Comm Mkt Stud, Sept. 1973, pp. 78-103.
Describes and evaluates the 1969 Arusha Agreement.

31-3 GWYER, G. D. 'East Africa and three international commodity agreements; the lessons of experience'. Econ Dev & Cult Change, April 1973, pp. 465-76.
Examines the coffee, tea and sisal agreements. Concludes that small exporting countries are disadvantaged in formal commodity agreements and in the distribution of gains from them.

31-4 HOPCRAFT, PETER N. 'Outward looking industrialization: the promotion of manufactured exports from Kenya'. Mimeographed. IDS Disc P 141, Sept. 1972, 22 pp.
Kenya lacks the capacity to expand traditional exports, and foreign firms are motivated to seek profits through import substitution rather than use their international connections to export. A review of trade, tariff and exchange rate policies is necessary if industrial exports are to expand.

31-5 KESSEL, DUDLEY. 'Effective protection of industry in Tanzania'. EAER, June 1968, pp. 1-18.
Finds that effective rates of protection are generally higher than nominal rates and that they are highest for import substituting industries producing non-durable consumer goods.

31-6 KYESIMIRA, YOERI. Agricultural Export Development. East African Publishing House, Nairobi, 1969, 100 pp.
Concludes in favour of a strategy of diversifying the range of agricultural exports.

31-7 LEWIS, STEPHEN R. (JR.) The Effects of Protection on the Growth Rate of the Economy and on the Need for External Assistance. IDS Working paper No. 34, April 1972, 19 pp.

(LEWIS, STEPHEN R. (JR.))
Incorporates the effects of protection into a 'two-gap' projection model, and examines some dynamic implications.

31-8 NDEGWA, P. 'Preferential trade arrangements among developing countries'. EAER, Dec. 1965, pp. 1-22.
Looks at possible trade links between East Africa and other less developed economies.

31-9 SZARF, A. AND MUSIC, D. 'Informal commodity arrangements: the case of Tanzanian sisal'. FAO Monthly Bulletin of Agricultural Economics and Statistics, March 1970, pp. 1-7.
Describes the salient features of the arrangements and developments leading to their implementation.

32 - Balance of payments experiences and policies

32-1 CARTER, A. G. T. 'The balance of payments of East Africa, 1956-1961; with comments on current trends'. EAER, Dec. 1963, pp. 75-87.
A general survey, including discussion of the relation between balance of payments and the general economy.

32-2 RESNICK, IDRIAN N. 'Tanzania's foreign reserve position'. EAER, June 1967, pp. 85-90.
Concludes that external reserve policies ought to be based upon the judgement of the central bank, rather than being legislated.

32-3 VINNAI, VOLKER. 'The system of exchange control in Kenya'. IDS Disc P 148, Sept. 1972, 25 pp.
Presents the legal framework of the exchange control system; looks at the role of the Foreign Investment Protection Act, and suggests improvements.

32-4 YAFFEY, M. J. H. Balance of Payments Problems of a Developing Country: Tanzania. Weltforum Verlag, Munich, 1970, 290 pp.
Analyses Tanzania's terms of trade, international investments, and other elements of the balance of payments.

33 - Foreign investments and aid

33-1 CLARK, RALPH; SOPER, TOM and WILLIAMS, PETER. Aid in Uganda - Programmes and Policies. Overseas Development Institute, London, 1966, 101 pp.
Demonstrate distorting effects of donor-tied aid and recommend project-tied aid.

INTERNATIONAL TRADE

33-2 COHEN, D. L. and TRIBE, M. A. 'Suppliers' credits: Ghana and Uganda'. J Mod Afr Studs, Dec. 1972, pp. 525-541.
Suppliers' credit and contractor finance as an imperialist technique with results unfavourable to Ghana and Uganda.

33-3 GITELSON, SUSAN A. 'How are development projects selected? The case of the UNDP in Uganda and Tanzania'. The African Review, 1972, No. 2, pp. 365-380.
Explores interactions between the politicians and civil servants of the recipient governments and officials of aid agencies in selecting aid projects.

33-4 HERMAN, B. 'Some basic data for analysing the political economy of foreign investment in Kenya'. Mimeographed. IDS Disc P 112, July 1971, 19 pp.
Discusses sources and size of foreign investment in Kenya, use of local savings and employment of local partners.

33-5 JACOB, ABEL. 'Foreign aid in agriculture: introducing Israel's land settlement scheme to Tanzania'. African Affairs, April 1972, pp. 186-194.
Argues that both economic and social factors should be evaluated by donors and recipients before co-operative aid enterprises are launched.

33-6 Kenya, Republic of, and United Nations Development Programme. Mobilising for Progress. Nairobi, 1967, 54 pp.
Discusses the contribution of the United Nations Development Programme to Kenya's development.

33-7 LAL, DEEPAK. Appraising Foreign Investment in Developing Countries. Heinemann Economics, London, 1974, 224 pp.
Presents guidelines for appraising investments and contains case studies of cost-benefit analysis in India and Kenya, with consideration of the non-economic factors involved.

33-8 LANGDON, STEVEN. 'Multinational corporations, taste transfer and underdevelopment: a case study from Kenya'. Review of African Political Economy, 1975, No. 2, pp. 12-35.
A study of the Kenyan soap and detergent industry, pointing out the serious shortcomings of multinational corporations as institutions of technology transfer.

33-9 MAKONI, T. 'The economic appraisal of the Tanzania - Zambia railway'. The African Review, 1972, No. 4, pp. 599-616.

(MAKONI, T.)
Compares benefits of the interest-free Chinese loan with a hypothetical Western loan of equal magnitude and studies the trade reorientation that will result from the railway.

33-10 METTRICK, H. Aid in Uganda - Agriculture. Overseas Development Institute, London, 1967, 135 pp.
Gives details of bilateral and multilateral aid to 1966, and establishes criteria for aid projects and methods of channelling funds.

33-11 MORGAN, DAVID JOHN, ed. British Private Investment in East Africa: Report of a Survey and Conference. Overseas Development Institute, London, 1965, 63 pp.
Surveys issues and problems involved in development in East Africa and the provision of capital and expertise to the area.

33-12 NEERSON, PETER. 'Tanzania's policies on private foreign investment'. The African Review, 1974, No. 1, pp. 61-78.
Tanzania has attempted to combine public control with efficiency by the use of para-statal corporations and foreign managers.

33-13 NEWMAN, PETER. 'Foreign investment and economic growth: the case of East Africa, 1963-1970'. EAER, Dec. 1964, pp. 22-39.
Using a Chenery/Bruno-type model, projects net public and private capital inflow requirements to 1970.

33-14 RASMUSSON, RASMUS. Kenyan Rural Development and Aid. Swedish International Development Authority, Stockholm, 1972, 53 pp.
Examines effects of external assistance on planning and implementation of the rural development programme.

33-15 _____. On Optimal Assistance, with Special Reference to the Second Kenyan and Tanzanian Five-year Plans. Center for Afro-Asian Research, Budapest, 1973, 100 pp.
An assessment of the foreign aid necessary for implementation of the plans.

33-16 SHARKANSKY, I. and DRESANG, D. L. 'International assistance: its variety, co-ordination and impact among public corporations in Kenya, and the East African Community'. International Organisation, 1974, pp. 207-231.

INTERNATIONAL TRADE

33-17 SHIVJI, ISSA G. 'Capitalism unlimited: public corporations in partnership with multinational corporations'. The African Review, 1973, No. 3, pp. 359-382.
Explores partnership relations between public and multinational corporations in Tanzania, concluding that partnership with foreign investors results in loss of control of vital economic resources.

33-18 SINGER, H. W. and DOSS, A. C. 'Technical assistance to Kenya: some thoughts on flows and programming'. EAER, June 1969, pp. 17-28.
Examine magnitude and direction; argue that programming is necessary to identify priorities and speed up development.

33-19 SMITH, HADLEY E., ed. Problems of Foreign Aid. Oxford University Press, Nairobi, 1965, 289 pp.
A collection of papers on various aspects of development aid to East Africa.

33-20 TANDON, YASHPAL, ed. Technical Assistance Administration in East Africa. Almqvist and Wiksell, Stockholm, 1973, 209 pp.
A collection of papers which emphasize advance planning of technical assistance in order to avoid administration problems.

33-21 United Kingdon, Ministry of Overseas Development. Aid Policy in One Country: Britain's Aid to Kenya, 1964-68. Mimeographed. London, 1970, 16 pp.
Argues that British aid had the objective of an orderly change from colonial status to independence, as reflected in aid for land settlement, agrarian reform and technical assistance for the civil service.

33-22 VAN ARKADIE, BRIAN and NDEGWA, PHILIP. 'Future trade, balance of payments and aid requirements in East Africa'. EAER, June 1965, pp. 32-64.
Analyse factors determining the amount of foreign aid necessary to achieve desirable rates of growth in 1965-1970.

33-23 VOCI, J. J. and STONER, J. A. F. 'The reality of technical assistance'. International Development Review, 1967, No. 4, pp. 10-16.
Examine technical assistance to the cashew nut processing industry in Tanzania.

33-24 WILLIAMS, PETER. Aid in Uganda: Education. Overseas Development Institute, London, 1966, 152 pp.
Shows that about 80% of Uganda's secondary school teachers were from overseas; Makerere University College was largely financed by outside funds; and many Ugandans on higher studies were in overseas institutions.

34 - East African co-operation: general and historical

34-1 HAZLEWOOD, ARTHUR, ed. African Integration and Disintegration: Case Studies in Economic and Political Union. Oxford University Press, London, 1967, 414 pp.
Includes 'Economic Integration in East Africa' by Hazlewood. Deals with the experience and problems of economic integration in East Africa in the 1960's with special emphasis on the common market and common services.

34-2 LEYS, COLIN AND ROBSON, P. Federation in East Africa: Opportunities and Problems. Oxford University Press, Nairobi, 1965, 244 pp.
Explore the possible economic consequences of political union in East Africa.

34-3 NEWLYN, W. T. 'Monetary systems and integration'. EAER, June 1964, pp. 41-58.
Clarifies the relationship between political and economic integration, with special reference to monetary aspects, applied to the East African situation.

34-4 NIXSON, F. I. Economic Integration and Industrial Location: An East African Case Study. Longmans, London, 1973, 181 pp.
Considers the forces which have conditioned the concentration of industry in certain areas not immediately apparent as suitable. Includes a case study of location in Uganda.

34-5 NYE, J. S. 'East African economic integration'. J Mod Afr Studs, Dec. 1963, pp. 475-502.
Argues that economic integration is a pre-condition of federation.

34-6 _____. Pan-Africanism and East African Integration. Harvard University Press, Cambridge, Mass., 1965, 309 pp.
Discusses the effect of ideology upon integration in 1960-64.

INTERNATIONAL TRADE

34-7 O'CONNOR, A. M. 'A wider Eastern African economic union? Some geographical aspects'. J Mod Afr Studs, Dec. 1968, pp. 485-493.
Argues that East African economic integration is hindered by the unequal distribution of natural resources and benefits, language and currency restrictions.

34-8 PEARSON, SCOTT R. and PAGE, JOHN M. 'Redistribution of industry in the East African common market'. OIES Bull, Nov. 1971, pp. 275-288.
Investigate the problem of redistributing net gains in a regional grouping of less developed economies.

34-9 ROBSON, P. 'The reshaping of East African economic co-operation'. EAJ, Aug. 1967, pp. 3-10.
Argues that integration should enable regions to take advantage of economies of scale and specialisation, with regional gains equitably distributed.

34-10 ROTHCHILD, DONALD, ed. Politics of Integration, An East African Documentary. East African Publishing House, Nairobi, 1968, 343 pp.
A general survey of attempts to form an East African federation. Includes one section on the Common Market.

34-11 SEIDMAN, ANN. Problems and Possibilities for East African Economic Integration. Mimeographed. African Studies Association, Boston, 1970, 17 pp.
Argues that to achieve economic integration the East African countries must control the regional institutions necessary to plan and carry out a strategy of industrial and agricultural growth.

34-12 United Nations. Co-operation for Economic Development of Eastern Africa. (9 parts). Department of Economic and Social Affairs, New York, 1971, pp. 37, 51, 24, 102, 54, 33, 105, 26, 40.
Includes separate studies of co-operation in industry, agriculture, energy, transport, human resources, and trade.

34-13 WIONCZEK, M. S. 'Economic integration and regional distribution of industrial activities: a comparative study. Part 2: East Africa'. EAER, June 1967, pp. 31-43.
Draws attention to the difficulty of devising economically and politically acceptable schemes for allocating industry within a regional grouping like the East African Community.

35 - The East African Community

35-1 CHAUD, S. Welfare and the East African Common Market: Some Observations. Central Planning Bureau, Statistics Division, Entebbe, Jan. 1966, 16 pp.
Discusses the production effect of the common market and its importance in assessing the gains and losses incurred by members of a customs union.

35-2 DI DELUPIS, INGRID DOIMI. The East African Community and Common Market. Longman, London, 1970, 185 pp.
Analyses the functions of the Community, the common market, and its association with the European Economic Community.

35-3 East African Common Services Organization. Development Plan for the Period 1-7-64 to 30-6-70. Government Printer, Nairobi, 1964, 137 pp.

35-4 East African Community Central Secretariat. 'Summary and guide to some of the main provisions for East African co-operation'. Econ Stat Rev, March 1967, pp. VIII-XVII.
A summary of the text of the treaty.

35-5 ELKAN, WALTER and LESLIE, N. 'The economic links between Kenya, Uganda and Tanzania'. Mimeographed. IDS Disc P 143, 1972, 24 pp.
Examine the institutions of East African co-operation and the allegation that Kenya gains most from the Community.

35-6 GHAI, DHARAM P. 'State trading and regional economic integration: the East African experience'. J Comm Mkt Stud, 1974, No. 3, pp. 296-318.
Investigates the impact of the growth of state trading enterprises on the operation of the East African common market.

35-7 _____. 'Territorial distribution of benefits and costs of the East African common market'. EAER, June 1964, pp. 29-40.
Develops a theoretical framework to analyse the distributional effects of a common market and applies it to the East African common market.

35-8 GREEN, REGINALD H. Economic Union in East Africa: Principles, Prices and Proceeds. Mimeographed. East African Institute of Social Research Conference Proceedings, Part A, Jan. 1966, 41 pp.

INTERNATIONAL TRADE

(GREEN, REGINALD H.)
Discusses the quota system, industrial licensing, common market and currency issues, concluding that an economic union which is not based on a policy structure consonant with that of its member states cannot be successful.

35-9 HAZLEWOOD, ARTHUR. 'The East African Common Market: importance and effects'. OIES BULL, Feb. 1966, pp. 1-18.
A general discussion of the common market, and the volume and limitations of inter-territorial trade.

35-10 _____. Economic Integration: The East African Experience. Heinemann, London, 1975, 172 pp.
Traces the history of East African co-operation and the development of the Community; discusses unsettled problems and future prospects. Concludes that the partner states will have to take positive decisions if the Community is to survive.

35-11 _____. 'The Kampala Treaty and the accession of new members to the East African Community'. EAER, Dec. 1968, pp. 49-63.
Argues that the Treaty makes it impossible for additional countries to accede to the Community and suggests amendments to remedy this.

35-12 _____. 'Notes on the treaty for East African co-operation'. EAER, Dec. 1967, pp. 63-80.
Examines provisions in the treaty affecting agriculture, labour relations, credit and the Development Bank.

35-13 _____. 'State trading and the East African Customs Union'. OIES Bull, May 1973, pp. 75-89.
Argues that the growth of state trading bodies has been the most important change in the economic environment under the 1967 treaty for East African Co-operation, and discusses the implications.

35-14 _____. 'The territorial incidence of the East African common services'. OIES Bull, Aug. 1965.

35-15 HELLEINER, G. K. Transfer Taxes, Tariffs and the East African Common Market. Mimeographed. ERB paper 67/16, Nov. 1967, 10 pp.
Examines the economic implications of the transfer tax provisions of the Treaty for East African Co-operation.

35-16 KAKOZA, JOSEPH. 'The common external tariff and development in the East African Community'. Finance and Development, March 1972, pp. 22-30.
Concludes that the common tariff has aided industry in East Africa.

35-17 MASSELL, BENTON F. The Distribution of Gains in a Common Market: The East African Case. Rand Corporation, Santa Monica, California, 1964, 23 pp.

35-18 _____. East African Economic Union: An Evaluation and Some Implications for Policy. Rand Corporation, Santa Monica, California, Dec. 1963, 94 pp.
Examines the contribution that economic integration makes to development in East Africa, and suggests some measures to improve the performance of the common market.

35-19 MEAD, DONALD C. 'Economic co-operation in East Africa'. J Mod Afr Studs, July 1969, pp. 227-287.
Explores the prospects for economic co-operation as outlined in the 1967 Treaty.

35-20 NDEGWA, PHILLIP. The Common Market and Development in East Africa. East African Publishing House, Nairobi, 1965, 228 pp.
Examines the contribution of inter-country trade among the three East African countries to their economic development.

35-21 NEWLYN, W. T. 'Gains and losses in the East African Common Market'. Yorkshire Bulletin of Economic and Social Research, Nov. 1965.

35-22 OUKO, ROBERT. 'A review of the East African common market in 1971'. Econ Stat Rev, June 1972, pp. VIII-XXIII.
Reviews developments within the common market, and its functions.

35-23 PROCTOR, J. H. and KRISHNA, K. G. V. 'The East African Common Services Organization: an assessment'. South Atlantic Quarterly, 1965, No. 4, pp. 526-48.

35-24 ROE, A. R. 'Terms of trade and transfer effects in the East African common market: an empirical study'. OIES Bull, Aug. 1969, pp. 153-169.
Analyses national terms of trade within the Customs Union and the new system of transfer taxes.

THE AGRICULTURE SECTOR

35-25 SEGAL, AARON. 'The integration of developing countries: some thoughts on East Africa and Central America'. J Comm Mkt Stud, March 1967, pp. 252-282.
A comparative study of the East African Economic Union and the Central American Common Market.

35-26 SVOBODA, JERRY L. 'Transfer tax and the Development Bank: a new look for the East African Community'. African Law Studies, Nov. 1969, pp. 93-102.
Argues that the Bank finances development in all the partner states whereas the transfer tax favours Tanzania and Uganda.

4 - THE AGRICULTURAL SECTOR

40 - Structure and organisation

40-1 Kenya, Central Bureau of Statistics. 'Kenya agricultural census, 1963'. K Stat Dig, Dec. 1963, pp. 1-2.
Observations on provisional results for the scheduled areas and coastal strip.

40-2 Kenya, Ministry of Finance and Economic Planning. Report of the Working Party on Agricultural Inputs. Sir Wilfred Havelock, Chairman. Government Printer, Nairobi, 1971, 62 pp.
Examines the costs of agricultural inputs such as fertilizers and machinery. Recommends government policies on distributional and credit facilities.

40-3 McLOUGHLIN, PETER F. M. Agriculture in East and Central Africa; An Overview. Longmans, London, 1970, 59 pp.
Includes an assessment of agriculture in Kenya, Uganda and Tanzania, with projections to 1978.

40-4 _____. 'East African economic development over the next twenty years: some forecasts about qualitative changes'. Canadian Journal of African Studies, 1971, No. 2, pp. 227-240.
Discusses influences on the future nature, pace and direction of the agricultural and industrial sectors.

40-5 STOCES, FERDINAND. 'Place of agriculture in the East African economy, 1955-1963'. Agricultural Economics Bulletin for Africa, Addis Ababa, 1967, pp. 79-104.

(STOCES, FERDINAND)
Examines labour absorption in agriculture, its share in total exports and its contribution to gross domestic product.

40-6 U.N. Economic Commission for Africa. 'Agriculture in the East African Sub-Region'. Econ Bull Afr, 1969, pp. 1-49.
A broad examination of East African agriculture and its development.

40-7 OPIO-ODONGO, J. M. A. 'Agricultural productivity in Uganda; a special organizational perspective'. EAJ Rural Devel, 1975, Nos. 1 and 2, pp. 118-128.
Studies critically the problems of modernization in agriculture in terms of the impact of the organization of social units (districts) on agricultural productivity, and examines the relative impact of several different social organizational dimensions.

41 - Sample, locality and farm studies

41-1 ALDINGTON, T. J. and SMITH, L. D. 'The Mwea Irrigation Scheme and rice marketing in Kenya'. EAJ Rural Devel, 1971, No. 1, pp. 16-44.
Argue that the scheme is production- rather than market-orientated, and discuss faults in the marketing system.

41-2 ATTEMS, M. Peasant Farms in the Tropical Highlands of East Africa. Weltforum Verlag, Munich, 1967, 170 pp.
An agro-economic analysis of farms in Shambalaland, Tanzania.

41-3 BARNES, CAROLYN. 'The introduction of coffee in Gusiiland, Kenya, 1933-1942'. IDS Disc P 205, July 1974, 27 pp.
Part of a broader study. By 1938, many of the farmers were willing to grow coffee, but expansion was halted by government policy of limiting coffee production by Kenyan Africans.

41-4 BERNARD, F. E. East of Mount Kenya: Meru Agriculture in Transition. IFO, Munich, 1975, 176 pp.
Assesses changes in crops, animals, land tenure, settlement and agricultural techniques in Meru during colonial and post-independence eras.

THE AGRICULTURE SECTOR

41-5 BERRY, LEN and KATES, R. W. Planned Irrigated Settlement: A Study of Four Villages in Sodona and Singida Regions, Tanzania. University College, Dar-es-Salaam, 1970, 63 pp.

41-6 BULLOCK, RONALD A. 'Subsistence to cash: economic change in rural Kiambu'. Cahiers d'Etudes Africaines, 1974, No. 4, pp. 699-714.
Argues that economic change has resulted in an inversion of economic status between northern and southern Kiambu in the last 50 years.

41-7 CHAMBERS, R. AND MORIS, J. R., eds. Mwea: An Irrigated Rice Settlement in Kenya. Weltforum Verlag, Munich, 1973, 529 pp.
Analyse settlement life, the technical and production systems, administration and the problems of rice marketing and consumption in Kenya.

41-8 CLAYTON, ERIC S. Economic Planning in Peasant Agriculture: A Study of the Optimal Use of Agricultural Resources by Peasant Farmers in Kenya. Department of Agricultural Economics, Wye College, (University of London), 1963, 69 pp.
Shows how the best use of land, labour and capital can be achieved by peasant farmers to maximise farm productivity.

41-9 COLLINSON, M. P. The Economic Characteristics of the Sukuma Farming System. Mimeographed. ERB paper 72/5, Sept. 1972, 47 pp.
Shows how the Sukuma have improved their standard of living through farming.

41-10 _____. 'Experience with a trial management farm in Tanzania'. EAJ Rural Devel, 1969, No. 2, pp. 28-43.
A study of the planning and results of Ukiriguru farm (near Mwanza) in 1962-65.

41-11 DUE, JEAN M. 'They said it couldn't be done - two agricultural development projects in Kenya'. Canadian Journal of African Studies, 1970, No. 3, pp. 595-614.
Examines a smallholder tea project and the resettlement of Africans on European farms.

41-12 GOLKOWSKY, R. Irrigated Agriculture in Kenya: A Presentation of the Basic Relations Exemplified by the Mwea Irrigation Settlement. IFO, Munich, 1969, 149 pp.
Shows that Mwea settlement is functioning economically.

Sample, locality

41-13 HALL, MALCOLM. 'A review of farm management research in East Africa'. Agricultural Economics Bulletin for Africa, 1970, No. 12, pp. 11-24.
Examines research methodologies for farm management studies.

41-14 HARPER, MALCOLM, ed. Kenyan Smallholders: Their Attitudes and Problems. FAO, Rome, 1973.
A collection of small-farm case studies.

41-15 HEYER, JUDITH. Alternative Development Strategies for Lowland Machakos Farms. Makerere Institute of Social Research, Kampala, Dec. 1966, 17 pp.
Shows how linear programming analysis can be used to identify farm production constraints.

41-16 _____. 'An analysis of peasant farm production under conditions of uncertainty'. Journal of Agricultural Economics, 1972, No. 2, pp. 135-46.
Uses a linear programming model to study the impact of cotton on the traditional food crop system in Masii, Kenya.

41-17 _____. The Economics of Small-Scale Farming in Lowland Machakos. IDS Occasional Paper No. 1, April 1967, 82 pp.
Discusses the role of cotton, maize and traditional crops with emphasis on factors limiting their growth.

41-18 HUNT, D. 'The introduction of single-axle tractors on peasant farms in Masaka Division, Southern Uganda'. EAJ Rural Dev, 1975, Nos. 1 and 2.
Cost estimates indicate that these tractors were not economically viable.

41-19 HUNT, D. M. Growth versus Equity: An Examination of the Distribution of Economic Status and Opportunity in Mbere, Eastern Kenya. Mimeographed. IDS Occasional Paper No. 11, 1975, 61 pp.
Concludes that only relatively wealthy farmers can be expected to supply the necessary resources for, and carry the risks of, innovation, thus creating a tension between growth and equity objectives.

41-20 Kenya, Central Bureau of Statistics. Farm Economic Survey Reports. Government Printer, Nairobi.
A series of these reports were issued. Those appearing from 1963 are listed below. These reports present data on inputs, costs, output and profitability for the specific

THE AGRICULTURE SECTOR

(Kenya, Central Bureau)
crops important to the area being surveyed, intended for use by farmers and extension officers in farm management work.

No.	Locality and period covered	Publication details
12.	Molo and Mau Narok (1961-62)	March 1963, 65 pp.
13.	Rift Valley (1961)	April 1963, 114 pp.
14.	Trans-Nzoia (1962-63)	Oct. 1963, 51 pp.
15.	Elgeyo and West Pokot (1962) (examines the causes of contrasts between the two areas)	Dec. 1963, 65 pp.
16.	Uasin Gishu (1959-62)	Dec. 1963, 59 pp.
17.	Western Kenya (describes the system of recording and analysis used in production cost studies of large-scale farming)	Dec. 1963, 19 pp.
18.	Nandi (1962-63) (case studies)	Feb. 1964, 65 pp.
19.	Molo and Mau Narok (1959-62)	May 1964, 72 pp.
20.	Njoro (1958-61)	July 1964, 61 pp.
21.	Nyeri (1962)	Aug. 1964, 126 pp.
22.	Trans-Nzoia (1958-61)	March 1965, 63 pp.
23.	Nandi and West Pokot (1963-64)	1965, 89 pp.
24.	Nyeri (1963)	1966, 86 pp.
25.	Nyeri (1964)	1968, 64 pp.
26.	Nyanza (1963)	1969, 83 pp.
27.	*See* entry No. 45-19	
28.	Trans-Nzoia (1967-68/ 1970-71)	1972, 115 pp.

41-21 _____. 'Statistical studies of small-holder farming in Kenya'. *K Stat Dig*, Dec. 1966, pp. 5-9.
Presents information on number of holdings, crop acreage, livestock population and farm employment in Bungoma district.

41-22 Kenya, Ministry of Co-operatives and Social Services. *A Base-line Survey of Factors Affecting Agricultural Development in Three Areas of Kenya*. H. L. Naylor, Author. Marco Surveys, Nairobi, 1965, 48 pp.
Report on a survey carried out in Bomet, Kabondo and Samia on basis of interviews with random samples of farm household heads.
See also entry 41-47.

41-23 KING, KENNETH J. 'Development and education in the Narok district of Kenya: the pastoral Maasai and their neighbours'. African Affairs, Oct. 1972, pp. 389-407.
Outlines a 5-10 year plan for education to promote the development of Maasai-land.

41-24 KURURAGIRE, A. R. 'Land fragmentation at Rugarama, Kigezi'. Uganda Journal, 1969, No. 1, pp. 57-64.
Discusses effects of mechanization on fragmented land-holdings.

41-25 LE CLAIR, EDWARD E. JR. and SCHNEIDER, HAROLD K., eds. Economic Anthropology: Readings in Theory and Analysis. Holt, Rinehart and Winston, New York, 1968, 523 pp.
Includes: Schneider, 'Economics in East African aboriginal societies' and Massell, Benton F., 'Economic variations on a theme by Schneider'.

41-26 LORD, R. F. Economic Aspects of Mechanized Farming at Nachingwea in the Southern Province of Tanganyika. Her Majesty's Stationary Office, London, 1963, 191 pp.
Discusses the organisation and operation of farming patterns adopted by the Overseas Food Corporation and the Tanganyika Agricultural Corporation.

41-27 LUDWIG, H. D. Ukara - A Special Case of Tropical Land Use in the Lake Victoria Area. Weltforum Verlag, Munich, 1967, 251 pp.
Investigates how a system linking traditional hoe cultivation to livestock husbandry has evolved and created intensive cultivation.

41-28 MacARTHUR, J. D. 'Experience with farm management analysis techniques in Kenya'. EAJ Rural Devel, July 1968, pp. 22-32.
A discussion of farm business analysis and the preparation of production cost data.

41-29 _____. Some Economic Case Studies of African Farms in the Rift Valley Province, 1961. Farm Economic Survey Unit, Nakuru, 1963, 114 pp.
Reports results of an economic survey of mixed farming in the "White" Highlands.

41-30 MacPHERSON, G. and JACKSON, D. 'Village technology for rural development: agricultural innovation in Tanzania'. International Labour Review, Feb. 1975, pp. 97-118

THE AGRICULTURE SECTOR

(MacPHERSON, G. and JACKSON, D.)
Describe and analyse an ILO/UNDP project aimed at improving the implements most appropriate to the needs and constraints of small-scale farmers.

41-31 MILLMAN, R. 'Change and challenge on the Kano Plains of Western Kenya'. South African Geographical Journal, 1968, No. 1, pp. 55-64.
Evaluation of irrigation possibilities on the Kano plains.

41-32 MOOCK, PETER R. 'The Vihiga S.R.D.P. farm-level survey: a preliminary report of findings'. Mimeographed. IDS Disc P 111, June 1971, 75 pp.
A statistical presentation of data on an S.R.D.P. project involving 600 farmers at Vihiga, with an introduction and interpretive comments.

41-33 POSNER, R. 'Preliminary results of a survey of the labour force on mixed farms in Trans-Nzoia'. Mimeographed. IDS Disc P 57, Sept. 1967, 12 pp.
Showing the sources of labour in Trans-Nzoia, indicates that the area employs large numbers of agricultural labourers.

41-34 RAIKES, P. L. Peasant Wheat Production in Four Districts of Tanzania. ERB, 1970, 32 pp.
Looks at the relationship between the cultivation of wheat and other crops; also farming practices, general income levels and family size.

41-35 RAUM, O. F. The Human Factor in the Development of the Kilombero Valley. IFO, Munich, Dec. 1965, 56 pp.
Outlines anthropological problems to be overcome before hydro- and agro-economic plans can be carried out.

41-36 ROLING, NIELS; CHEGE, FRED; and ASCROFT, JOSEPH. 'Rapid development for Kenya's small farms'. Mimeographed. IDS Disc P 173, July 1973, 12 pp.
Using Tetu SRDP extension pilot project, briefly describe some results obtained from field experimentation, the objectives and strategy of the project, and its problems.

41-37 RUTHENBERG, HANS, ed. Smallholder Farming and Smallholder Development in Tanzania: Ten Case Studies. Weltforum Verlag, Munich, 1968, 360 pp.

(RUTHENBERG, HANS)
Investigates land use, crop and animal husbandry practices, and the productivity of farming, with emphasis on interactions between technical, economic and social aspects.

41-38 SAYLOR, R. G. 'Farm level cotton yields and the research and extension services in Tanzania'. EAJ Rural Devel, 1974, Nos. 1 and 2, pp. 46-60.
Compares the yield impact of practices utilized by farmers and those recommended by research stations, focusing upon the relationship between yields, planting period, plant density and ridging.

41-39 STROBEL, HERBERT, ed. An Economic Analysis of Smallholder Agriculture in the Kericho District (Kenya). Institute of Socio-economics of Agricultural Development, Berlin, 1973, 212 pp.
Analyses the economic situation, the use of loans, and the input-output relationships of farm enterprises with different production techniques.

41-40 UCHENDU, VICTOR C. and ANTHONY, K. R. M. Agricultural Change in Geita District, Tanzania. East African Literature Bureau, Nairobi, 1974, 79 pp.
Illustrate the critical role of planned change--a settlement programme and tsetse-fly eradication--in opening up opportunities for agricultural development.

41-41 ______. Agricultural Change in Teso District, Uganda. East African Literature Bureau, Nairobi, 1975, 115 pp.
A study of the impact of the introduction of ox-ploughs and cotton growing, and associated government activities, on the development of Teso's economy.

41-42 VAN HEKKEN, P. M. and VAN VELZEN, H. Land Scarcity and Rural Inequality in Tanzania: Some Case Studies from Rungwe District. Africa-Studiencentrum, Mouton, 1972, 127 pp.
Places special emphasis on social obstacles to the implementation of Ujamaa policies.

41-43 VON GAGERN, A. African Settlers and how they Organise their Life in the Urambo Scheme, Tanzania. Weltforum Verlag, Munich, 1969, 130 pp.
Discusses management of tobacco farms in the scheme, specifying its economic and social implications.

41-44 VON ROTENHAM, D. Land Use and Cattle Raising in Sukumaland, Tanzania. Springer Verlag, Berlin, 1965, 131 pp.

THE AGRICULTURE SECTOR

(VON ROTENHAM, D.)
Argues that though there has been innovation in cash cropping, livestock husbandry has hardly changed.

41-45 WATTS, E. RONALD. 'Agricultural extension in Embu district of Kenya'. EAJ Rural Devel, 1969, No. 1, pp. 63-81.
Describes the structure, functioning and effectiveness of extension work at the farmer level.

41-46 WILSON, F. A. 'Area measurement techniques: some observations on the methodology developed in Kenyan research into small farm economics'. Agricultural Economics Bulletin for Africa, Addis Ababa, 1967, pp. 53-63.
A guide for researchers in small farm economics.

41-47 WILSON, GORDON M. Rural Development Survey in Three Areas of Kenya. Ministry of Co-operatives and Social Sciences, Nairobi, 1968, 99 pp.
Compares the results of pilot projects in Samia, Kabondo and Bomet for 1965 and 1968.
See also entry 41-20.

41-48 WISNER, BENJAMIN and MBITHI, PHILIP M. 'Drought in Eastern Kenya: comparative observations of nutritional status and farmer activity at 17 sites'. Mimeographed. IDS Disc P 167, 1973, 28 pp.
Portray farm decision-making as an adjustment behaviour and relate this to environmental circumstances. Advocate government dry-land farming research and development programmes related to local adjustment patterns.

42 - Crop and livestock studies and policies

42-1 ACLAND, J. D. East African Crops. Longmans, London, 1971, 252 pp.
Discusses the production of field and plantation crops.

42-2 ALDINGTON, T. J. 'Producer incentives as a means of promoting agricultural development; a case study of cotton in Kenya'. Mimeographed. IDS Disc P 105, April 1971, 35 pp.
Concludes that cotton growers must receive higher incomes if the industry is to develop satisfactorily.

42-3 ALIBARUHO, G. 'Regional supply elasticities in Uganda's cotton industry and the declining level of cotton output'. EAER, 1974, No. 2, pp. 35-56.

(ALIBARUHO, G.)
Finds output to be fairly responsive to price, although elasticities vary from region to region. Higher prices would reverse the decline in output.

42-4 ALLANSON, G. and PHIPPS, R. H. 'Large scale commercial dairy farming in Uganda: a farm management case study'. EAJ Rural Devel, 1971, No. 2, pp. 21-35.
A general guide for farmers intending to start large scale dairy farming.

42-5 BELSHAW, D. G. R. Price and Marketing Policy for Uganda's Export Crops: The Reports of the Cotton and Coffee Committees 1966/67. Mimeographed. Makerere Institute of Social Research, Jan. 1968, 20 pp.
Criticises the committees' recommendations and discusses appropriate price and marketing policies for cotton and coffee in Uganda.

42-6 DAVIS, R. K. 'The trade-off between wildlife and livestock in one ranching area of Kenya'. EAJ Rural Devel, 1972, Nos. 1 and 2, pp. 73-80.
Argues that planned livestock development may have been pushed too far vis a vis wildlife enterprises.

42-7 DE RAUCOURT, B. 'Report on a study tour of the sisal producing regions in East and South Africa'. Cotton Fibres Tropical, Paris, 1967, No. 4, pp. 491-550.
Reviews sisal industries in localities in Kenya, Tanzania, Mozambique and South Africa, emphasizing smallholder production.

42-8 DOWKER, B. D. and MATHEWS, V. G. Report on the Kenya Maize Industry. Government Printer, Nairobi, 1963, 39 pp.

42-9 DUNBAR, A. R. The Annual Crops of Uganda. East African Literature Bureau, Kampala, 1969, 189 pp.
Deals with the problems of crop husbandry, and the science and practice of agriculture.

42-10 ETHERINGTON, DAN M. 'The calculation of smallholder tea yields in Kenya by multiple linear regression analysis'. Mimeographed. IDS Disc P 40, Dec. 1966, 6 pp.
Stresses the importance of accurate yield forecasts for planning. Obtains some significant results but emphasises that the work needs to be taken further.

THE AGRICULTURE SECTOR

42-11 ETHERINGTON, DAN M. 'Economies of scale and technical efficiency: a case study in tea production'. EAJ Rural Devel, 1971, No. 1, pp. 72-87.
A case study of the appropriate mode of organisation for agriculture.

42-12 _____. Smallholder Tea Production in Kenya: A Econometric Study. East African Literature Bureau, Nairobi, 1973, 151 pp.
Uses a production function technique for estimating the tea yields obtained by smallholder farmers in Kenya.

42-13 FRANK, CHARLES R. JR. The Sugar Industry in East Africa. East African Publishing House, Nairobi, 1965, 115 pp.
An analysis of some problems and policy questions relating to the expansion of the sugar industry in a developing economy.
See also article in EAER, Dec. 1963.

42-14 GROENEVELD, S. Problems of Agricultural Development in the East African Coastal Region. Weltforum Verlag, Munich, 1967, 124 pp.
Investigates the failure of coconut and cattle projects.

42-15 GUILLEBAUD, C. W. An Economic Survey of the Sisal Industry of Tanganyika. Nisbet & Co., Welwyn, England, 1966, 146 pp.
General account of the development of the sisal industry between 1957 and the first half of 1966.

42-16 GWYER, G. D. Perennial Crop Supply Response: The Case of Tanzanian Sisal. School of Rural, Economic and Related Studies, Wye College, Ashford, Kent, 1971, 46 pp.
Sisal's contribution to the economy; its agronomic characteristics; short- and long-term response to price; output projections and their policy implications.

42-17 HUTCHISON, H. G. 'Ranching in Tanganyika'. East African Agricultural and Forestry Journal. Jan. 1965, pp. 268-75.
Discusses commercial cattle-keeping on small ranches.

42-18 International Bank for Reconstruction and Development. Study of the Availability of Fattening Beef Breeding and Dairy Breeding Stock in East Africa, 1970-75. 1972, 63 pp.
Study carried out to determine livestock requirements and potential supplies for various governmental and private development programmes.

42-19 JESPERSEN, C. B. Paddy in Usanga Plains. Ministry of Agriculture, Dar-es-Salaam, 1973, 96 pp.
A farm management survey of rice production with policy proposals.

42-20 KARANI, H. 'Kenya's maize muddle'. EAJ, March 1966, pp. 3-10.
The production and marketing of maize: problems and government involvement.
See rejoinder by Y. Kyesimira in June 1966 issue, pp. 33-35.

42-21 KENNEDY, T. J. A Study of Economic Motivation Involved in Peasant Cultivation of Cotton. East African Institute of Social Research Conference Proceedings Part C, Jan. 1964, 8 pp.
Outlines steps to raise yields and income derived from cotton in the Nyanza and Coast Provinces of Kenya.

42-22 Kenya, Central Bureau of Statistics. 'Census of sugar cane production, 1966-70'. K Stat Dig, Sept. 1970, pp. 4-8.
Describes the census and provides production data relating to Nyanza Province, which covers 90% of total output.

42-23 Kenya, Ministry of Agriculture. Final Report of the Livestock and Meat Working Party. Mimeographed. I. Vukovich, Chairman. Nairobi, 1971, 17 pp.
Reviews present status of the industry, suggests a long-term strategy and recommends policies for the seventies.

42-24 Kenya, Republic of. Report of the Select Committee on the Maize Industry. Government Printer, Nairobi, June 1973, 45 pp.
Presents recommendations on price and production policies.

42-25 KIWUWA, G. H. 'The influence of management and season of calving on milk production in a herd of crossbred cattle in Central Uganda'. East African Agricultural and Forestry Journal, 1969, No. 3, pp. 332-339.
Investigates production characteristics and yields on crossbred heifers.

42-26 MacGILLIVRAY, SIR DONALD. East African Livestock Survey. F.A.O., Rome, 1967, 215 pp.
Covers various aspects of livestock industry as a preliminary to a textbook on the subject.

THE AGRICULTURE SECTOR

42-27 MACKENZIE, W. 'Conflicts and obstacles in livestock development in Tanzania'. EAJ Rural Devel, 1972, Nos. 1 and 2, pp. 81-102.
A discussion of constraints hindering the improvement of productivity of livestock in Tanzania.

42-28 MAITHA, J. K. Coffee in the Kenya Economy. East African Literature Bureau, Nairobi, 1974, 87 pp.
An econometric study employing a neo-classical production function to predict future output and supply elasticities. Includes chapters on the history of the industry and its role in the economy.
See also articles in EAER, June 1969 and December 1970.

42-29 _____. 'A note on distributed lag models of maize and wheat production response: the Kenyan case'. Journal of Agricultural Economics, May 1974, pp. 183-188.
Price elasticities show that large scale farmers are highly responsive to price changes.

42-30 MASSELL, B. F.; HEYER, JUDITH; and KARANI, H. 'Maize policy in Kenya'. IDS Disc P 20, Dec. 1965, 15 pp.
Discuss pricing and marketing problems, with particular emphasis on storage.

42-31 MEYN, K. Beef Production in East Africa. IFO, Munich, Aug. 1970, 230 pp.
Concludes that the expanding market, rising beef prices and availability of large areas suitable for ranching make beef production viable in East Africa.

42-32 MIRACLE, MARVIN. Maize in Tropical Africa. University of Wisconsin Press, Madison, Wisconsin, 1966, 327 pp.
Discusses the importance of maize food to the economies of tropical Africa. Includes a chapter on maize in Eastern Africa.

42-33 MPONCULIANA, R.; MWANIKI, J. J.; and ADEL, S. L. A Survey of the Sisal Industry in East Africa. Department of Economics, University of Nairobi, 1969, 15 pp.
Surveys the historical growth of production and marketing, and the future of the industry.

42-34 MUSIC, D. 'Tanzanian Sisal'. F.A.O. Monthly Bulletin of Agricultural Economics and Statistics, May 1969, pp. 1-8.
Concludes that only low cost sisal estates currently producing over 1,000 tons per year have a long-term future.

42-35 OGENDO, R. B. 'Kenya dairy industry'. Journal of Eastern African Research and Development, (two parts) 1971, No. 2, and 1972, No. 1, pp. 161-165; 41-67.
Part I discusses the historical background; part II describes the location and structure of the industry.

42-36 OLOYA, J. J. Coffee, Cotton, Sisal and Tea in the East African Economies. East African Literature Bureau, Nairobi, 1969, 87 pp.
A study of trends in the development of these export commodities in 1945-62.

42-37 PAYNE, W. J. A. 'The relationship between animal husbandry and human nutritional needs in East Africa'. East African Agricultural and Forestry Journal, July 1963, pp. 17-25.
Examines cattle rearing between 1948-58 in relation to population growth.

42-38 PEARSON, SCOTT R. and COWNIE, JOHN. Commodity Exports and African Economic Development, Lexington Books, Massachusetts, 1974, 285 pp.
Includes 'The role of cotton in Uganda's economic development' by Valimohamed Jamal.

42-39 PEARSON, SCOTT R. and MEYER, R. K. 'Comparative advantage among African coffee producers'. American Journal of Agricultural Economics, May 1974, pp. 310-313.
A comparative study of Ethiopia, Ivory Coast, Tanzania and Uganda.

42-40 POSSINGER, H. Sisal in East Africa: An Enquiry into Productivity and Profitability in the Peasant Economy. Springer Verlag, Berlin, 1967, 172 pp.
A case study of smallholder sisal and co-operative marketing.

42-41 SCHEFFLER, W. Supervised Peasant Production: An Example of Tobacco-Growing in Tanzania. Weltforum Verlag, Munich, 1967, 192 pp.
Examines the development of smallholder virginia tobacco.

42-42 SCHERER, F. The Development of Smallholder Vegetable Production in Kigezi, Uganda: Data, Observations and Experiences, Weltforum Verlag, Munich, Sept. 1969, 217 pp.
Concludes that the results of production and marketing of fresh vegetables show that marketing co-operatives are functional and viable.

THE AGRICULTURE SECTOR

42-43 SINGH, C. Report of the Maize Commission of Enquiry. Government Printer, Nairobi, 1969, 204 pp.
Discusses factors determining supply, demand, distribution and marketing of maize in Kenya.

42-44 STERKENBURG, JAN. Factors Determining the Growth of the Rungwe Coffee Industry. Mimeographed. Afrika-Studiencentrum, Leiden, Dec. 1970, 45 pp.
Traces coffee production in Rungwe District, Tanzania, from 1930 to present and relates it to coffee disease, price, productivity schemes and government policy. Concludes that production stagnated after 1960.

42-45 STERN, N. H. An Appraisal of Tea Production on Small-holdings in Kenya. Organisation for Economic Co-operation and Development, Paris, 1972, 134 pp.
An application of the Little-Mirrlees method of cost-benefit analysis to the third plan of the Kenya Tea Development Authority. Finds a high social rate of return.

42-46 TALBOTT, I. D. 'The development of Lamu cotton production prior to Kenya's independence'. EAJ Rural Devel, 1973, Nos. 1 and 2, pp. 19-38.
Historical survey of efforts to introduce cotton in Lamu district.

42-47 Uganda, Ministry of Agriculture and Co-operatives. An Economic Survey of Dairy Farming in Uganda. Government Printer, Entebbe, 1966, 76 pp.
A pilot study in Kyaggwe and Bugerere Counties of the production and consumption of milk from exotic cattle introduced in Uganda.

42-48 U.N. Development Programme. Beef Industry Development: Kenya. UNDP/FAO, Rome, 1971, 104 pp.
Studies meat processing costs at the Kenya Meat Commission in order to determine the optimum stock feeding and management techniques for increasing beef production. Based on work by G. Beddoes.

42-49 _____. East African Livestock Survey: Dairy Production and Marketing. S. Nielsen, Consultant. UNDP/FAO, Rome, 1966, 25 pp.
Discusses existing production, marketing and training arrangements and proposes a long-term plan for the development of the industry.
See also entries 42-48 and 42-50.

42-50 _____. East African Livestock Survey: Regional: Kenya, Tanganyika and Uganda. 3 vols. Donald MacGillivray, Consultant. UNDP/FAO, Rome, 1967, 215 pp.; 283 pp. Vol. I: Development Requirements; Vol. II: Development Plans; Vol. III: Atlas.
Investigates the opportunities and problems confronting the livestock industry and presents a plan for the further development of the industry.
See also entries 42-48 and 42-49.

42-51 U.N. Economic Commission for Africa. Prospects for Production, Marketing and Trade in Livestock and Livestock Products in Eastern Africa to 1985. 2 vols. Addis Ababa, 1972.

42-52 WALLACE, I. R. 'The development of the Meru coffee industry in Kenya'. EAJ Rural Devel, 1970, No. 2, pp. 30-56.
Suggests that an increase in the influence of the marketing sector is necessary.

42-53 WATERS, A. R. 'Change and evolution in the Kenya coffee industry'. African Affairs, April 1972, pp. 163-175.
Discusses institutional changes and the economic control structure in the coffee industry, 1900-70.

43 - Agricultural development experiences

43-1 BROOKE, C. 'Types of food shortages in Tanzania'. Geographical Review, 1967, No. 3, pp. 333-357.
Identifies five types of shortage based on physical, social and economic characteristics.

43-2 BROWN, L. H. Agricultural Change in Kenya: 1945-1960. Food Research Institute Studies, Stanford University, California, 1968, 57 pp.
Traces changes in the structure and organisation of production and output in response to economic conditions and government policies.

43-3 CLAYTON, ERIC S. Agrarian Development in Peasant Economies: Some Lessons from Kenya. Pergamon Press, Oxford, 1964, 154 pp.
Traces the development of, and problems in, Kenyan peasant agriculture in 1945-63.

43-4 DE WILDE, JOHN C. Experience with Agricultural Development in Tropical Africa. 2 vols. Johns Hopkins Press, Baltimore, 1967, 254 pp.; 466 pp.

THE AGRICULTURE SECTOR

(DE WILDE, JOHN C.)
Vol. II includes a Kenyan case study and a study of agricultural development in Sukumaland, Tanzania.

43-5 FELDMAN, D. and R. Co-operation and the Production Environment. Mimeographed. Rural Development Research Paper No. 100, Kampala, March 1970, 26 pp.
Explores economic and social factors affecting co-operation in agricultural production.

43-6 FORBES-WATT, D. 'Mechanized group farming in Uganda'. Land Reform, Land Settlement and Co-operation, 1968, No. 1, pp. 1-12.
Argues that the failure of mechanized schemes was due to neglect of past economic and social experiences.

43-7 FUGGLES-COUCHMAN, N. R. Agricultural Change in Tanganyika: 1945-60. Stanford Food Research Institute, Stanford University, 1964, 98 pp.
Surveys the development of Tanganyika's agricultural sector in the period.

43-8 HEYER, JUDITH. 'Origins of regional inequalities in smallholder agriculture in Kenya, 1920-1973'. EAJ Rural Devel, 1975, Nos. 1 and 2.
Summarises the agricultural development experiences of different districts, particularly with coffee, tea and dairying, and points out historical origins of current inequalities.

43-9 ILIFFE, JOHN. Agricultural Change in Modern Tanganyika. East African Publishing House, 1971, 47 pp.
Examines the pre-colonial background and stresses the complexity of the forces which caused the trend towards social differentiation and inequality.

43-10 JAMESON, J. D., ed. Agriculture in Uganda. Oxford University Press, London, 1970, 395 pp.
General topics on land use and agricultural development in Uganda since the 1930's.

43-11 JENSEN, WENDY. 'Agricultural development in East Africa: a review of 1967/1968'. EAJ Rural Devel, July 1968, pp. 72-88.
A review of performance in the East African countries, with emphasis on individual crop performance.

43-12 Kenya, Central Bureau of Statistics. 'A comparison of the intensity of cultivation on large and small farms in Kenya'. K Stat Dig, March 1972, pp. 4-9.
Concludes that smaller settlement farmers achieved higher yields than the large farmers in 1964-71.

43-13 OGUTU, M. A. 'The evolution of agrarian economy of East Africa, 1895-1960'. Journal of East African Research and Development, 1973, No. 2, pp. 167-190.
Concludes that the agrarian economy underwent radical change during the colonial years.

43-14 RUTHENBERG, HANS. Agricultural Development in Tanganyika. Springer Verlag, Berlin, 1964, 212 pp.
Discusses agricultural conditions in Tanzania and measures taken to encourage African peasant farming.

43-15 _____. African Agricultural Production Development Policy in Kenya, 1952-1965. Springer Verlag, Berlin, Jan. 1966, 164 pp.
Shows that, though expensive, agricultural development achieved notable rates of growth. Promotion of African farming and knowledge of costs and benefits are necessary.

43-16 SCHATZ, SAYRE P., ed. South of the Sahara: Development in African Economies. Macmillan, London, 1972, 363 pp.
Includes 'Productivity Change in Kenyan Agriculture', by Price, James E. (Describes the construction of an index of agricultural productivity for Kenya for the period 1954-66). Also includes 'Rural household expenditures in Kenya: consistent estimation of expenditure elasticities', by Massel, Benton F. (Presents a method for obtaining consistent estimates of the parameters in the Engel Curve relationship and applies the method to households in rural Kenya.)

43-17 SCHNEIDER, HAROLD K. 'Economic development and economic change: the case of East African cattle'. Current Anthropology, April 1974.
Argues that the opportunity costs for pastoralists of economic change tend to be much higher than for people whose wealth is principally in land, because of larger status losses.

43-18 SMITH, HADLEY E., ed. Agricultural Development in Tanzania. Oxford University Press, London, 1965, 119 pp.
A collection of brief papers on a wide variety of topics.

THE AGRICULTURE SECTOR

44 - Agricultural strategies and planning

44-1 AMANN, V. F., ed. Agricultural Policy Issues in East Africa. East African Agricultural Economics Society, Kampala, 1971, 341 pp.
A collection of papers arranged under the headings: I - general policy issues; II - crop policy issues and strategies; III - livestock policy in Uganda; IV - production and marketing policy issues; V - other issues related to policy.

44-2 BROWN, L. H. A National Cash Crops Policy for Kenya. Government Printer, Nairobi, 1963, 136 pp.
Indicates which crops it would be most beneficial to develop, and the best ways in which production could be increased. Also discusses marketing problems.

44-3 CHABALA, HERBERT H. A.; KIIRU, DAVID H. and MUKUNA, SOLOMON W. 'An evaluation of the programming and implementation management (PIM) system'. IDS Disc P 192, Jan. 1974, 25 pp.
A review of previous findings. Find PIM to be a valuable tool and recommend it for wider use.
See also entry 47-3.

44-4 CLAYTON, ERIC S. 'Agrarian reform, agricultural planning and employment in Kenya'. International Labour Review, Nov. 1970, pp. 431-453.
Concludes that higher unemployment will occur unless agricultural production is increased.

44-5 CLIFFE, LIONEL. 'Reflections on agricultural development in East Africa'. EAJ, Nov. 1965, pp. 26-35.
A discussion of the Kenya Government's Sessional Paper on African Socialism and its implications for agricultural policies.
See also entry 02-7.

44-6 CLIFFE, LIONEL et al. Socialist Transformation in Rural Tanzania: A Strategy for the Western Usambaras. ERB, Nov. 1969, 47 pp.
Argues that socialist agricultural development is viable, that co-operative agriculture prevents rural class differentiation and meets some of Tanzania's needs.

44-7 DUMONT, RENE. Tanzanian Agriculture after the Arusha Declaration. Ministry of Economic Affairs and Development Planning, Dar-es-Salaam, Oct. 1969, 62 pp.

(DUMONT, RENE)
A critique of agricultural and rural development policies in Tanzania.

44-8 ELLMAN, A. O. 'The introduction of agricultural innovations through co-operative farming: a brief outline of Tanzania's policies'. EAJ Rural Devel, 1971, No. 1, pp. 1-15.
Discusses a transformation approach to agricultural development, whereby investment and manpower are concentrated on groups of farmers settled in fertile parts of the country.

44-9 FELDMAN, D. 'An assessment of alternative policy strategies in the agricultural development of Tanzania and their application to tobacco farming in Iringa'. EAJ Rural Devel, 1970, No. 2, pp. 1-29.
Examines some experiences in agricultural policy in Tanzania particularly in improvement and transformation.

44-10 FORBES-WATT, DAVID. 'Work for progress and the recent design of agricultural development policy in Uganda'. EAER, 1966, pp. 49-64.
Examines and suggests remedies to agricultural policies in the 1966-71 Development Plan.

44-11 HALL, MALCOLM. 'Agricultural planning in Buganda, 1963-1966'. EAJ Rural Devel, 1968, pp. 52-69.
A description of agricultural planning and implementation in the Buganda Region.

44-12 HELLEINER, G. K., ed. Agricultural Planning in East Africa. East African Publishing House, Nairobi, 1968, 183 pp.
Proceedings of a 1967 conference. Part I contains papers on agricultural planning; Part 2 has papers on extension, settlement, mechanisation, credit and coffee.

44-13 HEYER, JUDITH. 'Kenya's agricultural development policy'. EAER, Dec. 1966, pp. 35-47.
Argues that the emphasis of Kenya's Plan is on areas of high potential for agriculture or for ranching, and tends to favour the progressive farmers.

44-14 _____. 'A linear programming analysis of constraints on peasant farms in Kenya'. Food Research Institute Studies, 1971, No. 1, pp. 55-67.

THE AGRICULTURE SECTOR

(HEYER, JUDITH)
Presents the results of a study focussed on identifying the major constraints, the way these influence farm systems, and the consequences of reducing or removing critical constraints.

44-15 _____. A Linear Programming Model for Peasant Agriculture in Kenya. East African Institute of Social Research, Jan. 1965, 13 pp.
Outline of a linear programming model for maximising production on peasant farms.

44-16 INUKAI, I. 'African socialism and agricultural development strategy: a comparative study of Kenya and Tanzania'. Developing Economies, March 1974, pp. 3-22.
Discusses the impact of colonialisation on Kenya's post-Uhuru policies; discussion of Tanzania focusses on recent policies.

44-17 JIWANI, S. H. M. 'Agricultural statistics and rural development planning in Uganda'. EAJ Rural Devel, 1973, Nos. 1 and 2, pp. 179-188.
A critical survey of the use of agricultural statistics in rural development planning with comments on availability and accuracy of data.

44-18 JOHNSEN, TOM. Small-holder Adaptation to Technological and Economic Change--Implications for Local Level Implementation of Development Plans; a Chagga Case. Mimeographed. Afrika-Studiecentrum, Leiden, Dec. 1970, 25 pp.
Shows the necessity of involving local population in planning processes so as to have a plan that fits the existing situation.

44-19 JOHNSTON, BRUCE F. 'The choice of measures for increasing agricultural productivity: a survey of possibilities in East Africa'. Tropical Agriculture, April 1964, pp. 91-113.
Stresses the need for increasing knowledge of both the technical possibilities for expanding output and the relative costs and returns associated with the available alternatives.

44-20 Kenya, Republic of. National Cash Crops Policy for Kenya. Government Printer, Nairobi, 1963, 135 pp.
Emphasizes expansion and diversification of cash crops coupled with self-sufficiency of foodstuffs.

44-21 LEAKEY, C. L. A. 'Factors affecting increased production and marketing of food crops in Uganda'. EAJ Rural Devel, 1971, No. 2, pp. 1-20.
Discusses the sequence of change that is needed to create conditions for real development of food production.

44-22 ODERO-OGWEL, L. A. 'Economic planning for peasant agricultural development under risk constraints'. EAJ Rural Devel, 1974, pp. 61-76.
Explores with application to Kenyan peasant agriculture the extent to which risk modifies decision-making based on perfect knowledge assumptions.

44-23 ODERO-OGWEL, L. A. and CLAYTON, ERIC. A Regional Programming Approach to Agricultural Sector Analyses: An Application to Kenyan Agriculture. Wye College, School of Economies and Related Studies, 1973, 88 pp.
Records results of a study to expose the difficulties and shortcomings of sector analysis.

44-24 STOCES, FERDINAND. 'Agricultural production, productivity and investments in the Development Plans of East African countries'. Agricultural Economics Bulletin for Africa, May 1969, pp. 1-26.
Discusses planned agricultural development in relation to population growth, labour productivity and investment.

44-25 _____. 'Notes on current plans for development of agriculture in East Africa'. Agricultural Economics Bulletin for Africa, Addis Ababa, July 1968, pp. 1-26.
Compares the emphases in the three countries: Kenya focuses on land resettlement and its attendant problems; Tanzania on land tenure reforms and under-employment; and Uganda is concentrating on farm diversification.

45 - Land use, resettlement, and tenure

45-1 ADEGBOYE, RUFUS O. 'Customary land tenure systems in Uganda'. Land Reform, Land Settlement and Co-operation, 1971, No. 1, pp. 68-73.

45-2 APTHORPE, R., ed. Land Settlement and Rural Development in Eastern Africa. Transition Books, Kampala, 1968, 102 pp.
A collection of papers on various aspects of land settlement, with case studies.

THE AGRICULTURE SECTOR

45-3 BARBER, WILLIAM J. 'Land reform and economic change among African farmers in Kenya'. Econ Dev Cult Change, Oct. 1970, pp. 6-24.
An analysis of the programme of land tenure reform launched in 1954.

45-4 BELSHAW, D. G. R. An Outline of Resettlement Policy in Uganda, 1945-63. Mimeographed. East African Institute of Social Research Papers, Kampala, June 1963, 19 pp.
Examines changes in resettlement policy and discusses proposals for future government action.

45-5 BIEBUYCK, D., ed. African Agrarian Systems. Oxford University Press, London, 1963, 407 pp.
Discusses land rights and land use in Africa with reference to technical, economic and administrative factors. Includes: Homan, F. D. 'Land consolidation and redistribution of population in the Imenti sub-tribe of the Meru (Kenya)'.

45-6 BROCK, BEVERLEY. 'Customary land tenure, "individualization" and agricultural development in Uganda'. EAJ Rural Devel, 1969, No. 2, pp. 1-27.
Critical analysis of the relationship between land tenure and agricultural development; concludes that 'ownership-fixation' alone does not lead to agricultural prosperity.

45-7 CHAMBERS, ROBERT. Settlement Schemes in Tropical Africa. Routledge and Kegan Paul, London, 1969, 294 pp.
A study of eight countries including Kenya, Tanzania and Uganda. Suggests how administrative difficulties can be anticipated and planned for in development projects. Includes an administrative case history of the Mwea irrigation settlement scheme in Kenya.

45-8 CLOUGH, R. H. 'Some notes on a recent economic survey of land settlement in Kenya'. EAER, Dec. 1965, pp. 78-83.
Criticises Etherington, D. M. article in EAER, June 1963 on land resettlement in Kenya.
See entry 45-12.

45-9 DAVIS, ROBERT K. 'Some issues in the evolution, organisation and operation of group ranches in Kenya'. EAJ Rural Devel, 1971, No. 1, pp. 22-33.
Methods of bringing pastoral rangelands into commercial production.

45-10 DE VOS, ANTOON AND JONES, TELWYN, eds. 'Proceedings of the symposium, July 1967, on wildlife management and land use'. East African Agricultural and Forestry Journal, June 1968, (special issue).
Papers relating to the value of wildlife in East Africa and problems of managing wildlife as a important form of land-use.

45-11 ELLMAN, A. O. 'Kitete--a land settlement scheme in northern Tanzania'. Land Reform, Land Settlement and Co-operatives, 1967, No. 1, pp. 12-21.
Summarises planning and implementation problems.

45-12 ETHERINGTON, D. M. 'Land resettlement in Kenya; policy and practice'. EAER, June 1963, pp. 22-34.
Reviews the general framework within which Kenya's land settlement schemes must operate if they are to be economically successful.
See also Clough, R. H., entry 45-8.

45-13 FLIEDNER, H. Land Tenure Reform in Kenya. Springer Verlag, Berlin, 1965, 114 pp.
Traces the history of land reform. Examines the results of 1954 legislation and concludes that future prospects depend on the attitudes of Africans, a majority of whom in a 1962 opinion poll were in favour of reform.

45-14 HARBESON, JOHN W. 'Land reforms and politics in Kenya, 1954-70'. J Mod Afr Studs, Aug. 1971, pp. 231-251.
An analysis of two major land reforms, viewed against their political and agrarian background. Concludes that two classes have emerged: the landed and the landless.

45-15 _____. Nation-building in Kenya: The Role of Land Reform. Northwestern University Press, 1973, 367 pp.
Investigates the inter-relationships of land reform, economic development, and political modernisation in Kenya before and after independence.

45-16 HARTY, W. J. Report to the Government of Tanzania on Village Settlement Scheme and Farmers Training Centre at Mlale. FAO, Rome, 1968, 19 pp.

45-17 HEADY, HAROLD F. Range Management in East Africa. Government Printer, Nairobi, 1972, 125 pp.
Surveys major problems of the use of range-lands and suggests possible solutions.

THE AGRICULTURE SECTOR

45-18 JAMES, R. W. Land Tenure and Policy in Tanzania. East African Literature Bureau, Dar-es-Salaam, 1971, 375 pp.
A critical and historical analysis, including a survey of trends in land tenure policy.

45-19 Kenya, Central Bureau of Statistics. An Economic Appraisal of the Settlement Schemes, 1964/65-1967/68. Mimeographed. Farm Economic Survey Unit Report No. 27, Nairobi, 1971, 165 pp.
Summarises the results of a series of farm management surveys undertaken on settlement schemes in 1964-68.

45-20 _____. 'An economic survey of settlement schemes, 1964-1965'. K Stat Dig, June 1966, pp. 2-7.
Assesses progress by analysing expenditures on inputs, production, employment, land-use, capital investment and cash incomes of new settlers.

45-21 Kenya, Republic of. Report of a Mission on Land Settlement in Kenya. Mimeographed. Brian Van Arkadie, Chairman. Nairobi, Dec. 1966, 295 pp.
An enquiry into the economic, sociological and administrative experience of Kenya's land settlement, especially the 'million-acre' scheme. Includes many recommendations on future policies.

45-22 LANDELL-MILLS, PETER M. 'On the economic appraisal of agricultural development projects: the Tanzania village settlement schemes'. Agricultural Economics Bulletin for Africa, Dec. 1966, pp. 1-36.
Discusses and evaluates the scope of village settlements, policies pursued, and administration of the programme.

45-23 LANGLANDS, B. W. A Preliminary Review of Land Use of Uganda. Makerere University, Department of Geography, 1971, 219 pp.
Classifies patterns of land use and provides detailed information by county.

45-24 LONGHURST, W. M. and HEADY, H. F. Report of a Symposium on East African Range Problems. The Rockefeller Foundation, New York, 1968, 119 pp.
Conclude that, due to increasing population and protein deficiencies, the potential of range-land should be utilised in production of meat and other animal products.

45-25 MacARTHUR, J. D. 'Benefits of hindsight: aspects of experience in the high and low density settlement programmes in Kenya'. EAJ Rural Devel, 1975, Nos. 1 and 2, pp. 1-45.
Uses appraisal reports prepared for 1964 to 1968 to compare some aspects of settlement planning with the way schemes worked out in practice.

45-26 MacDONALD, A. S. 'Some aspects of land utilisation in Uganda'. East African Agricultural Journal, April 1963, pp. 147-156.
Argues that productivity per acre has remained stationary. More attention to land utilisation, husbandry and marketing will be necessary if rising demands are to be met.

45-27 McKAY, JOHN. 'A review of rural settlement studies for Tanzania'. East African Geographical Review, April 1968, pp. 37-49.
Analyses traditional systems relevant in implementing settlement policies and Ujamaa Vijijini.

45-28 McWILLIAM, M. D. 'Economic viability and the race factor in Kenya'. Econ Dev Cult Change, Oct. 1963, pp. 55-69.
An examination of the economic problems created by the Africanisation of the White Highlands.

45-29 MITCHELL, FRANK. 'The economic value of game-viewing as a form of land use'. IDS Disc P 53, July 1967, 13 pp.
Concludes that the pastoral areas studied will make a larger contribution to GNP if game-viewing is included among the uses to which the land is devoted.

45-30 NAVEH, Z. 'The need for integrated range research in East Africa'. Tropical Agriculture, April 1966, pp. 91-98.
Urges the application of an integrated socio-economic and agro-ecological approach to the problems of range development in semi-arid lands.

45-31 NOTTIDGE, C. P. R. and GOLDSACK, J. R. Million-Acre Settlement Scheme, 1962-66. Mimeographed. Department of Settlement, Nairobi, 1966, 58 pp.
Discusses the nature and organisation of the scheme, and the related work of the Department of Settlement.

45-32 ODINGO, R. S. The Kenya Highlands. East African Publishing House, Nairobi, 1971, 229 pp.
Examines land use and agricultural development during the period of European farming.

THE AGRICULTURE SECTOR

45-33 PRATT, D. Rangeland Development in Kenya. Ministry of Agriculture and Animal Husbandry, Nairobi, 1968, 29 pp.
Discusses factors affecting rangeland development and describes government policies.

45-34 SEGAL, AARON. 'The politics of land in East Africa'. Econ Dev Cult Change, Jan. 1968, pp. 275-296.
Argues that the approaches of the three East African governments to land tenure; investment in agriculture, and rural development strategy are a reflection of their differing conceptions of the political situation.

45-35 SIMPSON, M. C. Alternative Strategies for Rangeland Development in Kenya. Leeds University Press, 1973, 60 pp.
Discusses the determination of boundaries, acquisition of title to land and the provision of water supplies as prerequisites to range development.

45-36 SORRENSON, M. P. K. Land Reform in the Kikuyu Country. Oxford University Press, Nairobi, 1967, 266 pp.
A discussion of the land reform designed to replace the uncertain customary tenure by registered land titles, and comprising consolidation and registration. Its implementation was relatively rapid because of the detention of many Kikuyus.

45-37 THIMM, H. U. 'Back-to-the-land: aspects of land use policy in Kenya'. EAJ Rural Devel, 1973, Nos. 1 and 2, pp. 157-164.
Study of rural development programmes as means of allocating resources.

45-38 VON HAUGWITZ, H. W. and THORWART, H. Some Experiences with Smallholder Settlement in Kenya, 1963/64 to 1966/67. Weltforum Verlag, Munich, 1972, 104 pp.
Describe settlement procedures and investigate the economic standing of settlement farms, tracing the causes of success or failure.

45-39 WASSERMAN, GARRY. 'The independence bargain: Kenya Europeans and the land issue, 1960-62'. Journal of Commonwealth Political Studies, July 1973, pp. 99-120.
Reviews the political background to the introduction of the Million Acre Settlement Scheme.

45-40 WEST, HENRY W. Land Policy in Buganda. Cambridge University Press, New York, 1972, 260 pp.
Studies the influence of freehold land tenure introduced in 1900.

45-41 WHETHAM, EDITH. 'Land reform and resettlement in Kenya'. EAJ Rural Devel, 1968, No. 1, pp. 18-29.
Reviews the 'million acre' scheme and assesses the prospects for making the new farms into commercially successful enterprises.

45-42 WILSON, RODNEY J. A. 'Land control in Kenya's smallholder farming areas'. EAJ Rural Devel, 1972, Nos. 1 and 2, pp. 123-140.
An examination of the objectives of land control in Kenya's smallholder farming areas.

46 - Agricultural extension, technologies, price policies

46-1 ASCROFT, JOSEPH R.; CHEGE, FRED E.; KARIUKI, JOSEPH F.; and ROLING, NIELS G. 'Accelerating the flow of new ideas to rural people: a proposal for a pilot extension training project in Nyeri'. IDS Disc P 133, Nov. 1971, 48 pp.
Provide an overview of the development of the SRDP from 1965; report the results of a survey of a project in Tetu District; propose an experimental strategy for increasing incomes through improved techniques.

46-2 CLAYTON, ERIC S. 'Mechanisation and employment in East African agriculture'. International Labour Review, April 1972, pp. 309-334.
Assesses the effectiveness of various mechanisation programmes, and their income and employment impact.

46-3 COLLINSON, M. P. 'The evaluation of innovations for peasant farming'. EAJ Rural Devel, July 1968, pp. 50-59.
Demonstrates the importance of full analysis of the impact of possible farm improvements, and the importance of understanding the systems into which it is proposed to introduce them.

46-4 HELLEINER, G. K. 'Agricultural development plans in Kenya and Tanzania'. Rural Africana, 1971, No. 13, pp. 36-42.
Provides statistics and comparisons of planned and actual expenditures of the two governments.

46-5 _____. 'Agricultural export pricing strategy in Tanzania'. EAJ Rural Devel, Jan. 1968, pp. 1-17.
An examination of the recent Tanzanian experience with agricultural pricing policy.

THE AGRICULTURE SECTOR

46-6 LEONARD, DAVID K. 'Organisational structures for productivity in Kenyan agricultural extension'. IDS Disc P 154, Dec. 1972, 24 pp.
Examines three agricultural extension activities and discusses policies and strategies for improving performance of each. Proposes a mobile junior staff service and concludes that various reforms taken together might double the productivity of Kenya's agricultural extension workers.

46-7 _____. 'The social structure of the agricultural extension service in the Western Province of Kenya'. The African Review, 1972, No. 2, pp. 323-344.
Finds that distribution of extension is skewed in favour of wealthier farmers, accentuating rural inequality and preventing the dissemination of innovations. Provides a sociological explanation.

46-8 MAITHA, J. K. 'Demand for tractors in Kenya agriculture'. Journal of Eastern African Research and Development, 1973, No. 1, pp. 31-38.
Uses econometric techniques to explore the causes of mechanisation and its effects on employment on large farms.

46-9 MBITHI, P. M. 'Issues in the transfer of useful knowledge in agricultural development in Kenya'. Agricultural Administration, Oct. 1974, pp. 285-300.
Outlines major issues in production, adaptation and transfer of technical knowledge.

46-10 MBITHI, P. M. and WISNER, B. 'Drought and famine in Kenya: magnitude and attempted solutions'. Journal of Eastern African Research and Development, 1973, No. 2, pp. 113-143.
Studies the selection of farming technology in response to marginal farming conditions.

46-11 MORIS, JOHN and SAYLOR, GERALD, eds. Technical Innovation and Farm Development in East Africa. Mimeographed. Makerere University, Kampala, 1975, 409 pp.
A collection of readings relating to research, extension services and advice.

46-12 NELSON, R. E. A Baseline Survey of Uganda Agriculture. USAID and Ugandan Ministry of Agriculture and Forestry, Entebbe, 1970, 73 pp.
An evaluation of the Extension Saturation Project, providing information on farm and farmer characteristics, production, consumption patterns and extension contacts.

46-13 SMITH, LAWRENCE D. 'Resource allocation, income redistribution and agricultural pricing policies in Kenya'. Mimeographed. IDS Disc P 85, Nov. 1969, 17 pp.
Concludes that agricultural price policies are better employed to secure an optimal allocation of resources rather than as a device for redistributing income to the rural areas.

46-14 VAIL, DAVID. 'Induced farm innovation and derived scientific research strategy: the choice of techniques in developing smallholder agriculture in land abundant areas'. EAJ Rural Devel, 1973, Nos. 1 and 2, pp. 1-17.
A critical analysis of plant breeding research and farm mechanisation in East Africa.

46-15 _____. Report on the Evaluation of Four of the Initial Sixteen Extension Saturation Projects in Uganda. Mimeographed. Makerere Institute of Social Research, 1970, 90 pp.
Concludes that extension methods were effective but needed to be supplemented by other forms of assistance.

46-16 WATTS, E. RONALD. 'Reaching East Africa's farmers--a survey of recent efforts to increase the effectiveness of agricultural extension in Kenya, Uganda and Tanzania'. J Admin Overseas, April 1973, pp. 112-124.
An analysis of efforts made to accelerate agricultural development in East Africa.

47 - Rural and community development, Ujamaa

47-1 AWITI, A. 'Economic differentiation in Ismani, Iringa Region: a critical assessment of peasant response to the Ujamaa Vijijini Programme'. Afr Rev, June 1973, pp. 209-239.
Doubts whether the vijiji vya ujamaa programme will be able to transform the capitalist mode of production into a socialist mode without a clearer understanding of the meaning of socialism and self reliance.

47-2 BELSHAW, DERYKE and CHAMBERS, ROBERT. 'A management systems approach to rural development'. IDS Disc P 161, Jan. 1973. 28 pp.
Discuss past failures to plan rural development, and propose a simple system of rural plan management. Conclude that public sector performance in rural development is most likely to be improved through greater attention to programming, implementation and monitoring.

THE AGRICULTURE SECTOR

47-3 BELSHAW, DERYKE and CHAMBERS, ROBERT. 'PIM: a practical management system for implementing rural development programmes and projects'. IDS Disc P 162, Jan. 1973, 35 pp.
Describe the origins and operation of the PIM system. Argue that its employment could usefully be extended to assist the implementation of a variety of rural development programmes in Kenya and Tanzania.

47-4 BOLNICK, B. R. 'Comparative Harambee: history and theory of voluntary collective behaviour'. IDS Disc P 198, April, 25 pp.
Compares case studies of harambee activity in pre-independence America with Kenyan self-help. Conclusions are drawn for the more rational channelling of Harambee energies.

47-5 BROWN, BRACK E. S. Two Variables Affecting Rural Transformation in Kenya: The Settlement Case. Syracuse University, April 1967, 29 pp.
Describes and analyses how bureaucratic traditions and attitudes towards development projects affect institutional capabilities for achieving development in Kenya.

47-6 CAMERON, J. and DODD, W. A. Society, Schools and Progress in Tanzania. Pergamon Press, Oxford, 1970, 258 pp.
Discuss the impact of the industrialised West on rural communities and their incorporation into world-wide trade.

47-7 CHAMBERS, ROBERT. Managing Rural Development: Ideas and Experience from East Africa. Scandinavian Institute of African Studies, Uppsala, 1974, 216 pp.
Utilises East African experiences to make recommendations for other third world countries.

47-8 _____. 'Planning for rural areas in Africa: Experience and prescriptions'. The African Review, Jan. 1972, pp. 130-147.
Reviews decentralised planning with illustrations from Tanzania and Kenya.

47-9 CLIFFE, LIONEL. 'Planning rural development'. Development and Change, 1971-72, No. 3, pp. 77-98.
An analysis of the rural planning process in Tanzania emphasising its shortcomings.

47-10 CONNELL, JOHN. 'Ujamaa villages in rural Tanzania'. J Admin Overseas, Oct. 1972, pp. 273-84.
Reviews institutional changes.

47-11 ELLMAN, A. O. Progress, problems and prospects in Ujamaa development in Tanzania. ERB paper 70/18, March 1970, 35 pp.
Describes the Ujamaa policy, the problems encountered, and steps taken to overcome them.

47-12 FOSTER, PHILLIP and YOST, LARRY. Population Growth and Rural Development in Buganda: A Simulation of a Micro-Socio-Economic System. University of Maryland, 1968, 87 pp.

47-13 GEORGULAS, N. An Approach to the Economic Development of Rural Areas in Tanganyika with Special Reference to the Village Settlement Programme. Programme of East African Studies, Dar-es-Salaam, 1963, 47 pp.
Discusses the characteristics and implications of rural development policy and the significance of regional planning.

47-14 GHAI, DHARAM P., ed. 'Rural development in Kenya'. EAJ (special issue), March 1972, pp. 2-27.
Includes: Heyer, Judith 'Choice in the rural planning process'; Nellis, John 'The administration of rural development in Kenya'; Mbithi, Philip 'Issues in rural development in Kenya' and Gwyer, G. D. 'Employment opportunities in Kenyan agriculture'.

47-15 HEYER, JUDITH; IRERI, D.; and MORIS, J. Rural Development in Kenya. East African Publishing House, Nairobi, 1971, 132 pp.
Discusses the administrative, economic and social problems involved in developing rural areas, with particular reference to 14 divisions initially chosen for consideration for inclusion in the SRDP.

47-16 HUIZER, GERRIT. The Ujamaa Village Programme in Tanzania: New Forms of Rural Development. Institute of Social Studies, The Hague, May 1971, 30 pp.
Describes the Ujamaa programme, its achievements and problems.

47-17 INGLE, CLYDE R. 'Compulsion and rural development in Tanzania'. Canadian Journal of African Studies, 1970, No. 1, pp. 77-100.
Discusses implementation problems in stimulating change and development in north-eastern Tanzania.

THE AGRICULTURE SECTOR

47-18 INGLE, CLYDE R. From Village to State in Tanzania: The Politics of Rural Development. Cornell University Press, Ithaca, 1972, 279 pp.
Discusses the changes brought about by the Arusha Declaration, its interpretation and implementation by peasants.

47-19 Institute for Development Studies. An Overall Evaluation of the Special Rural Development Programme. Mimeographed. IDS Occasional Paper No. 8, 1973, 310 pp.
Prepared for the Kenya Government, the report includes a number of case studies as well as general discussion. Arrives at largely negative conclusions about the concept and implementation of the SRDP.

47-20 JUNOD, V. 'Community development and national planning: the Tanganyika case'. International Review of Community Development, Rome, 1966, pp. 165-178.

47-21 KEMPE, M. E. and SMITH, L. D. Strategies for Improving Rural Welfare. Mimeographed. IDS Occasional Paper No. 4, Nairobi, 1971, 562 pp.
A collection of brief papers on various topics, emphasising the decentralisation of planning, and co-ordination of rural education.

47-22 LEACH, J. W. 'The Kenya Special Rural Development Programme'. J Admin Overseas, April 1974, pp. 358-365.
Outlines the genesis and development of the SRDP, up to March 1973.

47-23 MBILINYI, SIMON M., ed. Agriculture Research for Rural Development. East African Literature Bureau, Nairobi, 1973, 247 pp.
Proceedings of the 6th Annual Symposium of the East African Academy, held in 1968. Includes papers on land tenure, physical environment potentials, and rural health.

47-24 _____. 'Rural development and rural employment generation: lessons from experimentation in Tanzania'. Rural Africana, 1973, No. 19, pp. 67-82.
Briefly analyses the traditional structure of the economy and problems of transformation in a socialist context.

47-25 MBITHI, PHILLIP. Rural Sociology and Rural Development: Its Application in Kenya. East African Literature Bureau, Nairobi, 1974, 229 pp.

(MBITHI, PHILLIP)
Includes coverage of such issues as labour migration, land tenure, Harambee self-help and community development. See also article in African Review, June 1972, and (with C. Barnes) IDS Disc P 204.

47-26 MORIS, JON R. Rural Development in Kenya. East African Publishing House, Nairobi, 1971, 132 pp.
Results of a survey measuring levels of rural development.

47-27 NELLIS, J. R. 'The administration of rural development in Kenya'. EAJ, March 1972, pp. 10-17.
Discusses the problems of producing plans and funds for the implementation of the SRDP.

47-28 _____. 'The planning of public support for Tanzanian rural development'. J Dev Areas, July 1967, pp. 477-488.
Discusses the village settlement programme as a scheme to bring scattered and landless people together to improve their productivity and standards of living.

47-29 NYERERE, J. K. Socialism and Rural Development. Government Printer, Dar-es-Salaam, 1967, 31 pp.
Stresses rural development through ujamaa villages.

47-30 O'BARR, JEAN F. Changes in Tanzanian Rural Society and their Relevance for Development Planning: a Seminar Report. Interuniversity Institute in the Netherlands, Leiden, Dec. 1973, 6 pp.
Contains annotated references to papers and case studies on Ujamaa and its implementation.

47-31 _____. Rural Development in Tanzania, the Political Dimension. Mimeographed. African Studies Association, Philadelphia, Nov. 1972, 15 pp.
Discusses programmes to improve rural standards of living.

47-32 ROHIO, S. 'Ideology and rural development'. EAJ, May 1972, pp. 29-31.
Discusses the social changes resulting from rural development in Kenya.

47-33 RWEYEMAMU, A. H. AND MWANSASU, B., eds. Planning in Tanzania: Background to Decentralisation. East African Literature Bureau, Nairobi, 131 pp.

THE AGRICULTURE SECTOR

(RWEYEMAMU, A. H. AND MWANSASU, B.)
Essays presented to a conference on Comparative Administration in East Africa in 1971, discussing aspects of rural development planning and its administration. See especially Collins, Paul: 'The working of Tanzania's Rural Development Fund: a problem in decentralisation'.

47-34 SMITH, CHR. Some Reflections on Rural Diversification (with Special Reference to the Coffee Areas on Mt. Kilimanjaro, Tanzania). Mimeographed. Afrika-Studiecentrum, Leiden, Dec. 1970, 37 pp.
Discusses rural reconstruction in which infrastructure has to change in conformity with national ideology, regional and natural potentials.

47-35 THURMANN, ULRICK, ed. Rural Development Administration in Bugoma District, Kenya. German Development Institute, Berlin, 1968, 165 pp.
Results of a study carried out in 1968. Presents: Ripkin, P. 'Problems of development administration in Bugoma District'; Harlmann, K. 'Rural and rural-urban water supply in Western Province'; Framhein, G. 'Adult education in Bugoma District'.

47-36 WATTS, E. R., ed. New Hope for Rural Africa. East African Publishing House, 1969, 151 pp.
Proceedings of a conference held at Kikuyu, Kenya in Sept. 1967. Concerned with how to effect rural development to combat rising unemployment, large numbers of school leavers and low agricultural productivity.

48 - Economic geography, natural resources, conservation, pollution

48-1 AMANN, HANS. Energy Supply and Economic Development in East Africa. Weltforum Verlag, Munich, 1969, 254 pp.
Surveys the physical, political and economic determinants of energy supply in East Africa, and the role of the energy sector in the region's economic development.

48-2 BAKWESEGHA, C. J. 'Patterns and processes of spatial development: the case of Uganda'. East African Geographical Review, April 1974, pp. 46-64.
Applies a modified version of Friedmann's "core-periphery" model to Uganda's development experiences.

48-3 CONYERS, DIANA. Agro-economic Zones of Northeastern Tanzania. Bureau of Resource Assessment and Land Use, University of Dar-es-Salaam, 1970, 123 pp.

48-4 LINEAR, MARCUS. The Conservation of Nature through the Rational Exploitation of Wildlife Resources. IFO, Munich, 1973, 105 pp.
Ecological-economic discussion of the advantages of wildlife promotion and cropping over beef production on marginal lands.

48-5 MORGAN, W. T. W., ed. East Africa: Its Peoples and Resources. Oxford University Press, Nairobi, 1972, 312 pp.
A completely revised version of E. W. Russell's 'Natural resources of East Africa'.

48-6 O'CONNOR, A. M. An Economic Geography of East Africa. Bell and Sons, London, 1966, 292 pp.
Examines economic activities and their distribution in East Africa, indicating the factors affecting the activities.

48-7 _____. 'Regional contrasts in economic development in Uganda'. East African Geographical Review, April 1963, pp. 33-43.
Attempts to indicate the nature of the spatial relationship between levels of prosperity within Uganda and the pattern of economic development at that time.

48-8 OJANY, F. and OGENDO, R. B. Kenya: A Study in Physical and Human Geography. Longmans, Nairobi, 1973, 228 pp.
Part II includes chapters on major sectors, population and industrial location.

48-9 OMINDE, S. H., ed. Studies in East African Geography and Development. Heinemann, London, 1971, 273 pp.
Collected essays on a variety of related topics.

48-10 SAFIER, M. 'Towards the definition of patterns in the distribution of economic development over East Africa'. East African Geographical Review, April 1969, pp. 1-13.
Analyses development at the regional, district and local levels.

48-11 SOJA, EDWARD W. The Geography of Modernisation in Kenya: A Spatial Analysis of Social, Economic, and Political Change. Syracuse University Press, New York, 1968, 143 pp.
Seeks to understand the interplay of forces which have shaped the human geography of Kenya. Argues that geographically uneven modernisation without systematic interdependence within a political area creates inequalities within the population that did not exist prior to the contact situation.

5 - THE INDUSTRIAL AND SERVICE SECTORS

50 - Industrial structure and organisation

50-1 BAILY, MARY ANN. 'Capital utilisation in Kenya manufacturing industry'. IDS Disc P 206, Aug. 1974, 20 pp.
A summary of a Ph.D. thesis. The major conclusion is that utilisation rates, and therefore the ratios of output and labour to capital stock, are sensitive to the factor-price ratio.

50-2 HOUSE, W. J. 'Market structure and industry performance: the case of Kenya'. Oxford Economic Papers, Nov. 1973, pp. 405-19.
Finds a positive relationship between gross margins and monopoly power and an inverse relationship between gross margins and export sales.

50-3 Kenya, Central Bureau of Statistics. Industrial Production Surveys of Large Scale Firms, 1964-66. Nairobi, Jan. 1971, 30 pp.
Covers private firms with 50 or more employees in mining, manufacturing and construction. Also includes some government or quasi-government bodies with enterprise functions.

50-4 _____. Kenya Census of Industrial Production. Nairobi, 1965, 157 pp.
Covers all establishments with five employees or more in mining, manufacturing, construction and power in 1963.

50-5 _____. 'Survey of industrial production, 1968'. K Stat Dig, June 1970, pp. 1-6.
Shows numbers of persons engaged, input and output, and ratios of gross product to output in mining and quarrying, manufacturing, and building and construction.

50-6 _____. 'Survey of industrial production, 1969'. K Stat Dig, Dec. 1971, pp. 5-9.
Presents data on size, structure and relative importance for manufacturing establishments employing 50 or more.

50-7 _____. 'Surveys of industrial production, 1970 and 1971'. K Stat Dig, June 1973, pp. 1-10.
Summary of results showing gross product, input and output, and location of mining, quarrying, manufacturing, building and construction sectors of the economy.

50-8 MAITHA, J. K. 'A note on returns to scale and the form of the production function'. EAER, 1974, No. 2, pp. 63-65.
Concludes that a Cobb-Douglas production function cannot be rejected for Kenyan manufacturing industries, implying a unitary elasticity of substitution and constant returns to scale.

50-9 MUREITHI, LEOPOLD P. 'The elasticity of substitution, returns to scale and firm size: an analysis of Kenya data'. Journal of Eastern Africa Research and Development, 1975, No. 2.
A comparative analysis of large and small firms, within a production function framework. Finds small firms more likely to create employment and further other development objectives.

50-10 National Christian Council of Kenya. Who Controls Industry in Kenya? East African Publishing House, Nairobi, 1968, 279 pp.
Report of a Working Party. Presents a factual statement and evaluation of the control and ownership of major industrial organisations, and makes recommendations for future policy.

50-11 OGENDO, R. B. Industrial Geography of Kenya. East African Publishing House, Nairobi, 1972, 308 pp.
Studies industrial structure and location, with special emphasis on agriculture processing and fabricating industries, and on questions of concentration and decentralisation.

50-12 PEARSON, D. S. Industrial Development in East Africa. Oxford University Press, Nairobi, 1969, 213 pp.
Examines the structure of industry in East Africa, factors in industrial development, and policy considerations.

50-13 RWEYEMAMU, J. F. The Historical and Institutional Setting of Tanzanian Industry. ERB paper 71/6, 1971, 104 pp.
Studies the spatial distribution of industrial establishments and employment, and the shares of various economic zones in the country's manufacturing activity.

50-14 _____. Underdevelopment and Industrialisation in Tanzania. Oxford University Press, Nairobi, 1973, 273 pp.
Analyses the impact of colonialism on the industrial structure and growth; makes suggestions for a socialist industrialisation strategy.
See also article in Development and Change, 1971-72, No. 3.

THE INDUSTRIAL AND SERVICE SECTORS

50-15 SCHAEDLER, KARL. Manufacturing and Processing Industries in Tanzania. IFO, Munich, 1969, 55 pp.
Analysis of medium- and large-scale industries in 1965/67.
See also entry 51-6.

50-16 STOUTJESDIJK, A. J. Uganda's Manufacturing Sector. East African Publishing House, Kampala, 1967, 101 pp.
A study of industrialisation in Uganda, analysing the structural organisation.

50-17 United Nations. Industrial Development in Africa. 2 parts. Industrial Development Organisation, New York, 1967, 307 pp.
Part II includes a chapter on Kenya.

51 - Industrialisation, import substitution

51-1 KIM, KWAN S. 'An interindustry comparison of the employment and balance of payments effects of import-substitution in Kenya'. EAER, 1974, No. 1, pp. 70-80.
Uses the 1967 input-output table to estimate the quantitative effects of import-substitution, for 23 sectors.

51-2 KRISHNA, K. G. V. The Industrial Sector in Kenya's Plan: Some Comments. Mimeographed. East African Institute of Social Research Conference Proceedings, Jan. 1965, 7 pp.
Evaluates the programme for industrial development in Kenya and tests for its consistency with the objectives outlined in the 1964-70 Development Plan.

51-3 MAITHA, J. K. 'Industrial production in Kenya'. Journal of Eastern African Research and Development, 1972, No. 1, pp. 79-84.
A brief review of the growth record of the manufacturing sector, 1954-70.

51-4 MAITRA, PRIYATASH. Import Substitution Potential in East Africa. Oxford University Press, Nairobi, 1967, 42 pp.
Attempts to estimate the potential and assess the viability of import-substituting industries in Kenya, Uganda and Tanzania.

51-5 PORTER, RICHARD C. 'Kenya's future as an exporter of manufactures'. EAER, 1974, No. 1, pp. 44-69.
Views Kenya's exports to its Community partners as a temporary by-product of their strategy of import

(PORTER, RICHARD C.)
substitution and not a result of an outward-looking manufacturing sector. Kenya is thus not developing an efficient and viable alternative to traditional exports.

51-6 SCHAEDLER, KARL. <u>Crafts, Small-scale Industries, and Industrial Education in Tanzania</u>. IFO, Munich, 1968, 264 pp.
Argues for increasing attention to crafts and small-scale industries as a solution to the need for greater industrial output and employment.
<u>See also</u> entry 50-15.

51-7 Uganda, Ministry of Commerce and Industry. <u>A Survey of the Manufacturing Industries, 1973</u>. Mimeographed. Kampala, Aug. 1974, 24 pp.
One of the few official publications dealing with the economy after the declaration of 'economic war'. Contains comparable data for 1971-73 on output, inputs and employment.

51-8 VAN ARKADIE, BRIAN. 'Import substitution and export promotion as aids to industrialisation in East Africa'. <u>EAER</u>, Dec. 1964, pp. 40-56.
Compares the two alternatives and the rates of growth that might be attainable from each.

51-9 VAN ZWANENBERG, R. M. A. <u>Aspects of Kenya's Industrial History</u>. Mimeographed. African Studies Association, Philadelphia, Nov. 1972, 26 pp.
Concludes that industries were encouraged in Kenya after 1945, resulting in import substitution by foreign-financed consumer-good industries.

<u>52 - Industry studies</u>

52-1 AGIK, MARTIN LUTHER; BESISIRA, ILYAS KISOKE; and KIGGUNDU, JOHN. <u>The Cement Industry in East Africa</u>. Department of Economics, University of Nairobi, April 1969, 10 pp.
A study of the organisation, sources of finance, and economic role of the industry.

52-2 BIENEFELD, M. A. <u>The Construction Industry in Tanzania</u>. Mimeographed. ERB paper 70/22, 1970, 81 pp.
Discusses the structure of the industry, the market for its output, and makes recommendations on organisation.

THE INDUSTRIAL AND SERVICE SECTORS

52-3 CARTER, A. G. T. 'The development of the hard fibre industry'. Econ Stat Rev, March 1966, pp. VIII-XII.
Briefly outlines the development and problems of the world's industry, including the East African producers.

52-4 COLES, DIANA M. S. The Vegetable Oil Crushing Industry in East Africa. Oxford University Press, Nairobi, 1968, 131 pp.
Examines the production of soft edible oils in Uganda, with a comparative analysis of the industry in Kenya and Tanzania.

52-5 HELMSCHROTT, H. Structure and Growth of the Textile and Clothing Industry in East Africa. IFO, Munich, 1969, 130 pp.
Analyses the textile and clothing industry on the basis of a survey of producers and opportunities for development. Finds that the East African common market was of great importance to the industry's growth.

52-6 KING, KENNETH J. 'Kenya's informal machine makers: a study of small scale industry in Kenya's emerging artisan society'. World Development, April/May 1974, pp. 9-28.
Discusses informal manufacture of bicycle parts and accessories.

52-7 McDOWELL, J. 'Development of high protein/high-calorie biscuits in Uganda using protein sources'. EAJ Rural Devel, 1973, Nos. 1 and 2, pp. 97-110.
A proposal for combating malnutrition.

52-8 MILLER, J. 'A report on a case study of the tinned fruit and vegetable industry'. Mimeographed. IDS Disc P 55, July 1967, 29 pp.
Assesses the efficiency of the industry in relation to government objectives and its dependence on protection.

52-9 REICHELT, HANS. The Chemical and Allied Industries in Kenya. Weltforum Verlag, Munich, 1967, 182 pp.

52-10 U.N. Development Program. East African Livestock Survey: Hides, Skins and Leather Industries. G. Van Hoorn, Consultant. UNDP/FAO, Rome, 1966, 8 pp.
Investigates the potential of the industry and makes recommendations for improvement.
See also entries 42-48/49/50.

52-11 U.N. Economic Commission for Africa. The Development of Rubber Goods Manufacture in the East African Sub-Region. Addis Ababa, 1965.

52-12 WELLS, J. The Construction Industry in East Africa. ERB paper 72/2, 1972, 28 pp.
Examines the development of the construction industry and argues that demand for its output is a function of development.

52-13 WILSON, GAIL. Owen Falls: Electricity in a Developing Country. East African Publishing House, Nairobi, 1967, 111 pp.
Analyses the demand for and supply of electricity, and its contribution to economic development in Uganda.

52-14 ZINS, RAYMOND. 'The East African energy balance: 1966-1974'. Econ Stat Rev, March 1974, pp. VIII-XLVI.
Analyses primary and secondary sources of energy produced, traded and consumed in East Africa in the period 1966-1972.

53 - Entrepreneurship; business finance and administration

53 1 CHILD, F. C. and KEMPE, M. E., eds. Small-Scale Enterprise. Mimeographed. IDS Occasional Paper No. 6, Nairobi, 1973, 157 pp.
Present papers prepared for a conference held in Feb. 1973. Includes a summary of the discussions and their policy implications.

53-2 DESAI, R. The Family and Business Enterprise among the Asians in East Africa. Mimeographed. East African Institute of Social Research Conference Proceedings, Jan. 1965, 6 pp.
Outlines the functions of the joint family system in business activities.

53-3 HARPER, MALCOLM. The African Trader--How to Run a Business. East African Publishing House, Nairobi, 1973, 143 pp.
Shows how to analyse and solve management problems in small East African businesses, illustrating with accounts of real business situations.

53-4 KAMAU, J. Problems of African Business Enterprise. Mimeographed. East African Institute of Social Research, Conference Proceedings, Jan. 1965, 6 pp.
Discusses constraints on African entrepreneurship and argues that the long-term solution is overall economic and social development.

THE INDUSTRIAL AND SERVICE SECTORS

53-5 MARRIS, PETER. 'The social barriers to African entrepreneurship'. J Dev Stud, Oct. 1968, pp. 29-38.
Uses Kenya's experiences to discuss socio-economic obstacles which African entrepreneurs face, such as illiteracy, inadequate skills and experience, and poor access to credit.

53-6 MARRIS, PETER and SOMERSET, ANTHONY. African Businessmen: A Study of Entrepreneurship and Development in Kenya. East African Publishing House, Nairobi, 1971, 288 pp.
Report the results of research among over a thousand Kenyan firms. Study their historical and social setting, their organisation, and policies to aid the development of such businesses.

53-7 POGSON, ERIC. Sources of Finance for African Businessmen, Milton Obote Foundation, Kampala, 1969, 86 pp.
Discusses domestic financial institutions and markets.

54 - Policies towards industry and private business

54-1 HARPER, MALCOLM H. 'A prototype experiment to test the possibility of a cost effective extension service for small scale general retailers'. Mimeographed. IDS Disc P 193, Jan. 1974, 22 pp.
Suggests a low-cost method of staffing an extension service of this type.

54-2 NIXSON, F. I. and STOUTJESDIJK, A. J. 'Industrial development in Kenya and Uganda development plans'. EAER, Dec. 1966, pp. 65-77.
Comparative analysis featuring the industrial structures, strategies and targets in the two new development plans.

54-3 POWER, JOHN H. 'The role of protection in industrialisation policy, with particular reference to Kenya'. EAER, June 1972, pp. 1-20.
Argues that Kenya's protective system is distorted in favour of import substituting consumer goods and against intermediate, capital and export goods, and that this conflicts with Kenya's stated policy objectives.

54-4 _____. 'Tax reform and industrialisation policy: a comment on recent development in Kenya'. IDS Disc P 170, July 1973, 12 pp.
Argues the need to reform Kenya's industrial protection system in order to promote employment and reduce inequities in the system.

54-5 REIMER, RICHARD. 'Effective rates of protection in East Africa'. EAER, Dec. 1971, pp. 31-47.
Shows effective rates of protection for Kenyan industries to range from very high positive to moderately high negative rates, and that high protection has fostered inefficiency rather than large profits.

54-6 ROE, ALAN R. 'The future of the company in Tanzanian development'. J Mod Afr Studs, April 1969, pp. 47-67.
Examines the implications of the policy of nationalising private enterprises.

54-7 THOMAS, P. A., ed. Private Enterprise and the East African Company. Tanzania Publishing House, Dar-es-Salaam, 1969, 283 pp.
A collection of essays examining the problems posed by the adoption by each of the East African states of company legislation evolved to meet the needs of a different society.

55 - Transport and communications

55-1 DIAMOND, PETER; MITCHELL, FRANK; and MUTURI, M. 'Report of the air freight study group'. Mimeographed. IDS Disc P 79, June 1969, 50 pp.
Conclude that expansion of capacity would permit lower air fares and freight rates, and promote tourism in Kenya.

55-2 FORBES-WATT, D. 'Railways in Uganda'. J Dev Studs, Jan. 1967, pp. 206-211.
A review article of A. M. O'Connor's Railways and Development in Uganda.
See entry 55 9.

55-3 HAZLEWOOD, A. Rail and Road in East Africa. Basil Blackwell, Oxford, 1964, 247 pp.
A survey of road and rail transport and its economic contribution.

55-4 HOFMEIER, ROLF. Transport and Economic Development in Tanzania. Weltforum Verlag, Munich, 1973, 363 pp.
Traces the historical development of the Tanzanian transport system, with particular reference to road transport, and evaluates its contribution to development.

55-5 HOYLE, B. S. and HILLING, D., eds. Seaports and Development in Tropical Africa. Macmillan, London, 1970, 272 pp.

THE INDUSTRIAL AND SERVICE SECTORS

(HOYLE, B. S. and HILLING, D.)
Includes Hoyle, 'The Emergence of Major Seaports in a Developing Economy: The Case of East Africa'.

55-6 KIRKPATRICK, C. H. 'Road-track costs and road-user taxation in East African Community'. Econ Stat Rev, Sept./Dec. 1972, pp. VIII-XVIII.
An examination of the relationship between revenues obtained from road-users and the maintenance costs incurred by the governments.

55-7 MKAMA, JUMANNE. Transport Planning in Tanzania: An Assessment. Bureau of Resource Assessment and Land Use Planning, University of Dar-es-Salaam, 1969, 62 pp.

55-8 O'CONNOR, A. M. 'New rail construction and the pattern of economic development in East Africa'. Institute of British Geographers, June 1965.
Studies three railway projects in East Africa and concludes that new railway construction will not necessarily stimulate development, especially in areas already served by roads and in which peasant agriculture is the main activity.

55-9 _____. Railways and Development in Uganda. Oxford University Press, Nairobi, 1965, 176 pp.
Assesses the influence of rail facilities on the distribution of economic activities in Uganda.
See also 55-2.

56 - Marketing, trading, co-operatives

56-1 ALDINGTON, T. J. and SMITH, L. D. 'The marketing of rice in Kenya'. Mimeographed. IDS Disc P 74, Nov. 1968, 29 pp.
The major faults of the marketing system are a) inadequate attempts to expand the rice market among African consumers, b) lack of control over costs, and c) non-use of the market as a source of finance. Make recommendations.

56-2 ALDINGTON, T. J. and WILSON, F. A. The Marketing of Beef in Kenya. Mimeographed. IDS Occasional Paper No. 3, Nairobi, Sept. 1968, 302 pp.
Discuss the role of the Kenya Meat Commission, its selling policies, government policies towards KMC, and projections of beef exports to 1975. Summarised in IDS Disc P. 70.

Marketing, trading

56-3 ALIBARUHO, GEORGE. 'The impact of marketing board policy on the level and variability of cotton producer prices in Uganda, 1945-1969'. <u>IDS Disc P 199</u>, March 1974, 25 pp.
Assesses the impact of the Link Marketing Board on the stability of farmers' prices and incomes. Concludes that intra-seasonal fluctuations were worsened but inter-seasonal fluctuations were reduced.

56-4 ALVIS, VANCE Q. 'The marketing of staple foodstuffs in Kenya'. <u>African Urban Notes</u>, Fall 1970, pp. 2-22.
Describes the classification and marketing of specific foods (maize, potatoes, bananas and beans) and discusses the efficiency of rural markets.

56-5 No Entry.

56-6 APTHORPE, RAYMOND. <u>Co-operatives and Rural Development in East Africa</u>. Africana Publishing Corporation, New York, 1970, 271 pp.
Surveys consumer, marketing and producer co-operatives in East Africa and their contribution to rural development.

56-7 APTHORPE, RAYMOND, ed. <u>Rural Cooperatives and Planned Change in Africa: Case Materials</u>. (Vol. IV) U.N. Research Institute for Social Service, Geneva, 1970, 361 pp.
Presents: Brett, E. A. 'Problems of cooperative development in Uganda'; Hyden, G. and Karanja, E. 'Cooperative and rural development in Kenya'; Long, N. 'Cooperative enterprise and rural development in Tanzania'.

56-8 BUNKER, STEPHEN G. <u>Forms and Functions of Government Intervention in a Uganda Cooperative Union</u>. African Studies Association, Denver, 1971, 39 pp.
A case study of the Bugisa cooperative union.

56-9 GOOD, CHARLES M. <u>Rural Markets and Trade in East Africa: A Study of the Functions and Development of Exchange Institutions in Ankole, Uganda</u>. Department of Geography, University of Chicago, 1970, 252 pp.
Describes and evaluates the functional role of market places as elements of exchange and distribution.

56-10 HARING, J. E.; CHRISTY, S.; and HUMPHREY, J. F. 'Marketing boards and price funds in Uganda 1950-60'. <u>Journal of Agricultural Economics</u>, Sept. 1969, pp. 345-356.
Investigate the economic effects of lint and coffee marketing boards and price assistance funds.

THE INDUSTRIAL AND SERVICE SECTORS

56-11 HAWKINS, H. C. G. Wholesale and Retail Trade In Tanzania: A Study of Distribution in East Africa. Praeger, New York, 1965, 168 pp.
Discusses marketing of consumer goods in Tanzania, with emphasis on problems of distribution.

56-12 HELLEINER, G. K. Agricultural Marketing in Tanzania: Policies and Problems. Mimeographed. ERB paper 68/14, 1968, 39 pp.
Discusses the economics of marketing and examines policy questions.

56-13 HYDEN, GORAN. 'Co-operative education and co-operative development: the Tanzanian experience'. Agricultural Administration, Jan. 1974, pp. 35-50.
Analyses the experiences and effects of co-operative education.

56-14 _____. Efficiency versus Distribution in East African Co-operatives. East African Literature Bureau, Nairobi, 1973, 254 pp.
Studies rural co-operation in East Africa, with special emphasis on management problems, and relationships with government in Kenya.

56-15 JONES, WILLIAM O. Marketing Staple Food Crops in Tropical Africa. Cornell University Press, Ithaca, 1972, 293 pp.
A comparative examination of the supply hinterlands of four African cities, including Nairobi.

56-16 KAINZBAUER, W. Trade in Tanzania. IFO, Munich, 1968, 239 pp.
Describes marketing and trade for various products of Tanzania, trade organisations, and the impact of government policies.

56-17 KARANJA, E. Rural Economic Development and Management: The Case of Co-operative Management in East Africa. Mimeographed. African Studies Association, Philadelphia, Nov. 1972, 22 pp.
Discusses management problems of co-operative marketing societies.

56-18 Kenya, Central Bureau of Statistics. 'Preliminary results of the survey of distribution, 1971'. K Stat Dig, June 1974, pp. 1-8.
Presents methods used and tables showing gross product, and inputs and outputs of small and large distributive establishments.

56-19 Kenya, Republic of. Co-operative Development Policy in Kenya. Government Printer, Nairobi, Sept. 1970, 10 pp.
Sets out a five-year policy programme to assist Kenya's small-holders, on such matters as credit, distribution of inputs, marketing and processing.

56-20 KLEMM, H. 'Some aspects of milk marketing in Kenya'. Mimeographed. IDS Disc P 21, Jan. 1966, 35 pp.
Presents a summary of the main problems facing the dairy industry.

56-21 KRIESEL, HERBERT C.; LAURENT, CHARLES K.; HALPERN, CARL; and LARZELERE, HENRY E. Agricultural Marketing in Tanzania: Background Research and Policy Proposals. Michigan State University, Dept. of Agricultural Economics, June 1970, 138 pp.
A study of agricultural marketing and marketing institutions, with special emphasis on maize and recommendations for future policies.

56-22 MARTIN, A. Marketing of Minor Crops in Uganda. Her Majesty's Stationery Office, London, 1963, 78 pp.
A factual study of the marketing of non-perishable African-grown and locally consumed produce.

56-23 MASCARENHAS, A. C. and MBILINYI, S. M. 'The orange trade of Dar-es-Salaam: a case study of risk-taking among peasant food producers'. EAJ Rural Devel, 1971, No. 1, pp. 1-21.
Examine responses of peasants to demand by urban consumers and show that farmers have shifted the risk of marketing oranges by renting out their trees.

56-24 MBILINYI, S. M. and MASCARENHAS, A. C. 'Bananas and the Dar-es-Salaam market'. EAJ Rural Devel, 1973, Nos. 1 and 2, pp. 55-77.
An organisational study.

56-25 NEWIGER, N. Co-operative Farming in Kenya and Tanzania. IFO, Munich, 1967, 157 pp.
A comparative study of co-operative farming in Kenya and Tanzania, and of government assistance and control.

56-26 OKEREKE, OKORO. The Economic Impact of the Uganda Co-operatives. East African Literature Bureau, Kampala, 1974, 137 pp.
Views co-operatives as an instrument of policy in pre-coup Uganda to gain control of agricultural marketing. Assesses their impact, problems and policy options. See also article in EAJ Rural Devel, July 1968.

THE INDUSTRIAL AND SERVICE SECTORS

56-27 OLOYA, J. J. 'Marketing Boards and post-war economic development policy in Uganda, 1945-1962'. Indian Journal of Agricultural Economics, 1968, pp. 50-58.

56-28 _____. 'Some aspects of the development of the co-operative movement in Uganda, 1957-67; capital structure and problems encountered'. Tropical Agriculture, 1968, No. 4, pp. 317-322.
Concludes that despite overstaffing and a world surplus, co-operatives have made progress in marketing, credit and group farming for coffee.

56-29 PATEL, H. D. and RIORDEN, E. B. 'Making the most of sisal exports: an analysis of prices paid to Tanganyika and Kenya'. EAJ Rural Devel, Jan. 1968, pp. 39-47.
An examination and explanation of the differences in sisal export values obtained by Kenya and Tanganyika.

56-30 PAULUS, M. The Co-operative System in Tanganyika and Uganda--Opportunities and Tasks. IFO, Munich, 1967, 156 pp.
Assesses the role played by co-operatives in the development of the two countries.

56-31 PRATT, W. Uganda Committee on the Marketing of Livestock, Meats, Fish and their Products in Uganda. Government Printer, Entebbe, 1969, 148 pp.
Studies the problems of marketing, processing and distribution, and their financial implications, with policy recommendations.

56-32 SCHERER, A. 'A case study of co-operative marketing of fresh vegetables among Uganda smallholders'. Agricultural Economics Bulletin for Africa, June 1970, pp. 25-34.
Examines the role of small-scale co-operatives.

56-33 SCHUBERT, BERND. 'Some considerations on methods for evaluating marketing systems for agricultural products'. EAJ Rural Devel, 1973, Nos. 1 and 2, pp. 39-54.
Attempts to develop a set of criteria for evaluating marketing systems.

56-34 SEIDMAN, ANN. 'State trading agencies and co-operatives in East Africa'. African Urban Notes, Fall 1970, pp. 35-58.
Compares some aspects of the marketing policies of Tanzania, Uganda and Kenya, and problems of co-operatives.

56-35 SPINKS, G. R. Marketing of Livestock and Meat in Kenya. FAO, Nairobi, April 1966, 143 pp.

(SPINKS, G. R.)
Assesses existing marketing facilities and estimates the potential market in East Africa. Also includes a feasibility study of locations and size of processing plants for livestock products.

56-36 Tanzania, United Republic of. Report of the Presidential Special Committee of Enquiry into the Co-operative Movement and Marketing Boards. J. A. Mhaville, Chairman. Government Printer, Dar-es-Salaam, 1966, 84 pp.
Reviews organisational structures and makes proposals for improvements.

56-37 TAYLOR, D. R. F. 'The internal trade of Fort Hall district, Kenya'. Canadian Journal of African Studies, Nov. 1967, pp. 111-122.
Argues that by facilitating the exchange of agricultural products, the local markets are playing an important role in the development of the area.

56-38 Uganda, Republic of. Report of the Committee of Inquiry into the Affairs of all Co-operative Unions in Uganda. Shafiq Arain, Chairman. Government Printer, Entebbe, 1967, 409 pp.
Examines the constitution, working and financial conditions of co-operatives, and makes recommendations.

56-39 U.N. Development Programme. Marketing of Livestock and Meat in Kenya. G. R. Spinks, Consultant. UNDP/FAO, Rome, 1966, 143 pp.
Assesses existing marketing arrangements and discusses future demands for the Kenyan livestock industry.
See also entries 42-48/49.

56-40 WESTERGAARD, POUL. Primary Societies' Marketing Costs: A Case Study and Some General Remarks, Mostly on Efficiency. ERB paper No. 69/6, 1969, 17 pp.
Discusses how efficiency in marketing co-operatives can be enhanced by education, control and incentives.

56-41 _____. Co-operatives in Tanzania, their Functions as Economic and Democratic Institutions--Some Economic Comments. ERB, 1970, 31 pp.
Argues that as well as marketing and distribution channels for agricultural products, co-operatives are a major instrument of rural development.

56-42 _____. 'Analysis of the accounts of the co-operative societies in Tanzania for the years 1967-1969'. EAJ Rural Devel, 1974, Nos. 1 and 2, pp. 122-156.

THE INDUSTRIAL AND SERVICE SECTORS

(WESTERGAARD, POUL)
Analyses the Co-operative Union of Tanganyika, and the Savings and Credit Union League, and finds annual net deficits and negative own capital.

56-43 WHETHAM, EDITH. Co-operation, Land Reform and Land Settlement. Plunkett Foundation for Co-operative Studies, London, 1968, 79 pp.
A report on surveys in Kenya, Uganda, Sudan, Ghana, Nigeria and Iran.

56-44 WIDSTRAND, CARL GOESTA, ed. Co-operatives and Rural Development in East Africa. Africana Publishing Corporation, New York, 1970, 271 pp.
Selected papers examining economic, political and sociological problems of co-operatives against the wider background of rural development. Also published, in abbreviated form, by Skandinavian Institute for African Studies under the title African Co-operatives and Efficiency (1972).

56-45 WILSON, FRANK A. 'Some economic aspects of the structure and organisation of small scale marketing systems--marketing of fruit and vegetables in Kenya'. Mimeographed. IDS Disc P 176, Sept. 1973, 25 pp.
Summarises main findings of six case studies. Investigates the internal marketing system under various headings, and analyses the role of government.

56-46 YOSHIDA, MASAO. 'Agricultural marketing reorganisation in postwar East Africa'. Developing Economies, Sept. 1973, pp. 244-271.

57 - Tourism

57-1 BHAGAT, HARKISHAN. 'Tourism and national development in Tanzania'. International Tourism Quarterly, 1974, No. 3, pp. 47-56.
Discusses the development of the tourist industry, its foreign exchange earnings, employment creation and other benefits.

57-2 DIAMOND, PETER. 'On the economics of Tourism'. EAER, Dec. 1969, pp. 53-62.
Attempts to show the difference between tourism and other international trade transactions. Argues that tourist demand is affected by the level of government services provided in addition to the prices tourists face.

57-3 Kenya, Central Bureau of Statistics. 'Nairobi airport tourist survey, September 1968-August 1969'. K Stat Dig, Dec. 1970, pp. 4-10.
Report of a survey into characteristics, length of stay and expenditures of tourists to Kenya.

57-4 _____. 'A new series of statistics of migration and tourism'. K Stat Dig, June 1968, pp. 2-6.
Utilises new data on days spent by tourists in Kenya to re-estimate their foreign exchange spendings in 1963-67.

57-5 _____. 'Visits and revisits--a new series of tourism statistics'. K Stat Dig, Dec. 1973, pp. 4-9.
Presents for the first time data on revisits from tourists visiting all three East African countries in 1971-72.

57-6 MITCHELL, FRANK. The Costs and Benefits of Tourism in Kenya. Kenya Tourist Development Corporation, Nairobi, Nov. 1968, 59 pp.
Evaluates the economic value of tourism to Kenya in 1966/67, and makes projections of tourist receipts and costs.

57-7 _____. 'The value of tourism in East Africa'. EAER, June 1970, pp. 1-21.
Argues that there are pecuniary and non-pecuniary consequences of tourism, and that if Kenya, Tanzania and Uganda engage in competition with each other this will lower benefits.

57-8 MYERS, NORMAN. 'The tourist as an agent for development and wildlife conservation: the case of Kenya'. International Journal of Social Economics, 1975, No. 1, pp. 26-42.

57-9 OSER, JACOB. 'Promoting tourism in Kenya'. EAJ, June 1965, pp. 5-14.
Discusses ways of expanding the tourist industry.

57-10 OUMA, JOSEPH, P. B. M. Evolution of Tourism in East Africa. East African Literature Bureau, Nairobi, 1970, 117 pp.
Reviews organisational developments, evaluates tourism, assesses service facilities for visitors and makes suggestions on the future development of the industry.

57-11 POPOVIC, VOJISLAV. Tourism in Eastern Africa. Weltforum Verlag, Munich, 1972, 208 pp.
Surveys the problems of tourism development in each of the Eastern African countries.

THE INDUSTRIAL AND SERVICE SECTORS

57-12 SHIVJI, ISSA G., ed. Tourism and Socialist Development. Tanzania Publishing House, Dar-es-Salaam, 1973, 97 pp.

57-13 WRIGHT, F. C. Tourism in East Africa: Report of an Economic Inquiry. Her Majesty's Stationery Office, London, 1963, 82 pp.
Discusses the tourist attractions of East African wildlife, the tourist inflow, and the contribution of tourism to the East African economies.

58 - Public corporations and other para-statals

58-1 BLUME, H. Organisational Aspects of Agro-Industrial Development Agencies. Weltforum Verlag, Munich, 1971, 239 pp.
Discusses the operations of para-statal development agencies for tea, cotton and palm-oil, utilising data from Kenya, Mauritius and Uganda.

58-2 DRESANG, D. L. and SHARKANSKY, I. Public Corporations in Single Country and Regional Settings: Kenya and the East African Community. Mimeographed. African Studies Association, Philadelphia, Nov. 1972, 30 pp.
Compares the opportunities of and constraints on single-country and regional public corporations.

58-3 GLENTWORTH, G. and WOZEI, M. 'The role of public corporations in national development in Uganda'. The African Review, Jan. 1972, pp. 54-90.
Case studies of the Uganda Development Corporation and Uganda Electricity Board.

58-4 HAGG, INGEMUND. Some State-Controlled Industrial Companies in Tanzania: A Case Study. Mimeographed. Scandinavian Institute of African Studies, Uppsala, 1971, 18 pp.
Explores the characteristics of enterprises owned jointly with foreign investors.

58-5 HARLANDER, H. and MEZGER, D. Development Banking in Africa: Seven Case Studies. Weltforum Verlag, Munich, 1971, 390 pp.
Includes Harlander, 'The Industrial and Commercial Development Corporation of Kenya'.

58-6 LOXLEY, JOHN and SAUL, JOHN S. 'Multinationals, workers and the parastatals in Tanzania'. Review of African Political Economy, 1975, No. 2, pp. 54-88.

(LOXLEY, JOHN and SAUL, JOHN S.)
Nationalisation has given control over a significant part of the industrial sector but decision-making in parastatals remains unplanned and unco-ordinated. Parastatals have remained closer to multinational corporations than to the workers.

58-7 MRAMBA, B. P. and MWANSASU, B. U. 'Management for socialist development in Tanzania: the case of the National Development Corporation'. The African Review, Jan. 1972, pp. 29-47.
Trace the development of the National Development Corporation, particularly changes since its inception in 1965.

58-8 PACKARD, PHILIP C. 'Corporate structure in agriculture and socialist development in Tanzania'. EAJ Rural Devel, 1972, Nos. 1 and 2, pp. 163-182.
A case study of parastatal organisations in the Tanzanian agricultural sector.

58-9 _____. 'Management and control of parastatal organisations'. Development and Change, 1971-72, No. 3, pp. 62-76.
Sets out the problems of, and requirements for, effective public corporations, socialist and efficient in character and responsive to Tanzanian society.

58-10 PENROSE, EDITH. 'Some problems of policy in the management of the parastatal sector in Tanzania: a comment'. The African Review, Jan. 1972, pp. 48-54.
Discusses problems related to objectives, the incentive system, and the locus of control in public enterprises.

58-11 RANIS, GUSTAV, ed. Government and Economic Development. Yale University Press, New Haven, 1971, 567 pp.
Includes Frank, Charles R. 'Public and private enterprise in Africa', who presents material on the Uganda Development Corporation and the Uganda Electricity Board.

58-12 VINNAI, VOLKER. 'The role of Development Finance Company of Kenya in the industrialisation process'. IDS Disc P 180, Nov. 1973, 16 pp.
Presents an analysis of the Company's operations and their results. Concludes that DFCK, as a commercial investment company pioneering risky ventures, is a failure.

6 - POPULATION, MANPOWER, TECHNOLOGIES

60 - Demographic characteristics, population growth and development, population policies

60-1 ANKRAL, E. M. and RADEL, D. J., eds. Family Planning. Ministry of Co-operatives and Social Services, Nairobi, 1969, 129 pp.
Proceedings of a seminar on inter-professional teamwork for the family. Emphasise the importance for Kenya's objectives of the development of its human resources.

60-2 BAKER, S. J. K. 'The population geography of East Africa'. East African Geographical Review, April 1963, pp. 1-6.
Studies the population distribution as at mid-1961.

60-3 BLACKER, J. G. C. 'Population growth in East Africa'. Econ Stat Rev, Sept. 1963, pp. VIII-XII.
Measurement and analysis of demographic trends in East Africa.

60-4 BLACKER, J. G. C. and SMITH, T. E. Population Characteristics of the Commonwealth Countries of Tropical Africa. Athlone Press, London, 1963, 72 pp.
Includes 'Population Growth and Natural Increase in Tanganyika and Uganda'.

60-5 CALDWELL, JOHN C. and OKONJO, C., eds. The Population of Tropical Africa. Longmans, London, 1968, 457 pp.
Includes Lury, D. A. 'Population data in East Africa' and Ominde, S. H. 'Some Aspects of Population Movement in Kenya'.

60-6 CRAMER, J. 'Some notes on the population of Kenya'. Mimeographed. IDS Staff Paper No. 109, Aug. 1971, 21 pp.
Presents and discusses data on densities by district, and alternative population projections.

60-7 EGERO, BERTIL and HENIN, ROUSHDI A., eds. The Population of Tanzania. Bureau of Statistics, Dar-es-Salaam, 1973, 292 pp.
Examine the implications of the 1967 population census results for the future development of Tanzania.

60-8 ETHERINGTON, D. M. 'Projected changes in urban and rural population in Kenya, and the implications for development policy'. EAER, 1965, pp. 65-83.

(ETHERINGTON, D. M.)
Indicates the significance of different rates of growth of urban and total population, and makes regional projections to 1990 for the African population.

60-9 Ford Foundation. Urbanisation in Kenya (2 vols.) Ford Foundation, New York, 1972, pp. 45, 19.
Includes Laurenti, Luigi, 'Urbanisation trends and prospects' and Gerhart, John, 'Rural development and urban growth'.

60-10 FORSTER, GEORGE M. and YOST, LARRY. 'A simulation study of population, education, and income growth in Uganda'. American Journal of Agricultural Economics, Aug. 1969, pp. 576-591.
Analyse how changes in birth and death rates affect population growth, and educational and economic development.

60-11 GACHUHI, J. MUGO. 'African youth and family planning knowledge, attitudes and practices'. Mimeographed. IDS Disc P 189, Jan. 1974, 13 pp.
Survey data show that most Kenyan youths knew about family planning and have favourable attitudes. The need to provide family planning education is discussed.

60-12 _____. 'Family planning in Kenya: Programmes and problems'. Mimeographed. IDS Disc P 175, Aug. 1973, 11 pp.
Describes population planning services under various headings; stresses the need for development of suitable curricula on population education.

60-13 HEISEL, D. F. 'Fertility limitation among rural women in Kenya'. IDS Disc P 62, Feb. 1968, 17 pp.
Survey results show that many women wish to limit their family size but lack knowledge of how to do so.

60-14 _____. 'Measuring current population changes'. Mimeographed. IDS Disc P 22, Jan. 1966, 11 pp.
Suggests ways of measuring changes and providing essential data in the light of a shortage of useable and reliable information.

60-15 HIRST, M. A. and LANGLANDS, B. W. Studies in the Population Geography of Uganda and Tanzania. Makerere University, Department of Geography, 1970, 65 pp.
Present population patterns, densities and other demographic statistics.

POPULATION, MANPOWER

60-16 Kenya, Central Bureau of Statistics. 'Demographic studies in the Central Bureau of Statistics'. K Stat Dig, March 1973, pp. 4-7.
Presents methods used to collect vital statistics and for analysing existing demographic data by the Demographic Studies Unit.

60-17 _____. 'The future growth of Kenya's population and its consequences'. K Stat Dig, June 1971, pp. 1-7.
Presents alternative projections of Kenya's population and discusses their implications for education and job-creation.

60-18 _____. Kenya Population Census, 1962 (3 vols.). Government Printer, Nairobi, 1964, 125 pp; 94 pp.; 119 pp.
Vol. I: Population census areas by sex and age group; Vol. II: Analysis by race, tribe and sex; Vol. III: Analysis of characteristics of African population.

60-19 _____. Kenya Population Census, 1969 (3 vols.). Government Printer, Nairobi, 1971, 123 pp.; 82 pp.; 73 pp.
Vol. I: Population by sex, area and density, tribe and nationality; Vol. II: Data on urban population by urban centre, sex, area, density, size, age and education; Vol. III: Data on education, relationship to household, birth place and marital status.

60-20 _____. 'Population growth and urbanisation in Kenya'. K Stat Dig, Sept. 1964, pp. 5-8.
Studies the increase in population of all races in towns and small urban areas between 1948 and 1962.

60-21 _____. 'Population growth in Kenya, 1948-62'. K Stat Dig, Sept. 1963, pp. 3-5.
Uses historical data to make population projections to the end of the century.

60-22 _____. 'Population projections by district, 1970-1980'. K Stat Dig, Sept. 1972, pp. 4-10.
Projections based on 1962 and 1969 census results.

60-23 Kenya, Ministry of Economic Planning and Development. Family Planning in Kenya. Government Printer, Nairobi, 1967, 45 pp.
Reproduces a report of the U.S. Population Council on Kenya's population problems. Recommends administrative and technical assistance for government population policies.

Demographic characteristics

60-24 LANGLANDS, B. W. The Demographic Conditions of Uganda as a Developing Country. Makerere University, Dept. of Geography, 1970, 48 pp.
Analyses the population characteristics of the African population.

60-25 LURY, D. A. 'African population estimates'. Econ Stat Rev, Sept. 1965, pp. VIII-XII.
A back projection of East African census results.

60-26 ____. 'Population data in East Africa'. Mimeographed. IDS Disc P 18, Jan. 1966, 20 pp.
An introduction and guide to the existing literature.

60-27 MOLNOS, ANGELA. Attitudes towards Family Planning in East Africa. IFO, Munich, 1968, 414 pp.
Surveys attitudes towards family planning, and the position and role of women in economic and social development in East Africa.

60-28 MORGAN, W. T. and SHAFFER, N. M. Population of Kenya: Density and Distribution. Oxford University Press, Nairobi, 1966, 36 pp.
Population and density by province, district and location.

60-29 NDETI, KIRUTA and KOESOBJONO, SANTO. 'The background to Kenya's population policy'. Journal of Eastern African Research and Development, 1973, No. 1, pp. 75-88.
Briefly discuss the evolution of Kenya's population and steps taken to implement a family planning programme.

60-30 OMINDE, S. H. and EJIOGU, C. H., eds. Population Growth and Economic Development in Africa. Heinemann, London, 1972, 421 pp.
Includes several contributions relating to population, migration, education, statistics and family planning programmes in East Africa.

60-31 Population Council. 'Population policies of African countries: Kenya'. African Population Newsletter, July 1971, pp. 14-21.
Summary of a 1965 report to Kenya government making recommendations on family planning programmes.

60-32 Tanzania, Bureau of Statistics. 1967 Population Census (5 vols.). Government Printer, Dar-es-Salaam, 1969, 342 pp.; 304 pp.; 490 pp.; 476 pp.; 270 pp.

POPULATION, MANPOWER

(Tanzania, Bureau of Statistics)
Vol. I: Statistics for Enumeration Areas; Vol. II: Statistics for Urban Areas; Vol. III: Demographic Statistics; Vol. IV: Economic Statistics (education, agriculture etc.); Vol. V: Census Methodology.

60-33 TURYAGYENDA, J. D. 'Overpopulation and its effects in the Gombolola of Buhara, Kigezi'. The Uganda Journal, Sept. 1964, pp. 127-133.
Stresses the negative effects of rapid population growth and urges the need for immediate remedial measures.

60-34 Uganda, Republic of. Report on the 1969 Population Census (4 vols.). Government Printer, Entebbe, 1971, 467 pp.; 95 pp.; 257 pp.; n.a. pp.
Vol. I: The population of Administrative Areas--giving population data by age-groups and sex; Vol. II: Administrative Report--giving a brief account of how the census was planned, administered and analysed; Vol. III: Additional tables--tabulation of nationality, birthplace, marital status and education, by race, age and sex; Vol. IV: Analytical report--results of a demographic analysis.

61 - The labour force; migration

61-1 BRANDT, HARTMUT; SCHUBERT, BERND and GERKEN, EGBERT. The Industrial Town as a Factor of Economic and Social Development: The Example of Jinja, Uganda. Weltforum Verlag, Munich, 1972, 451 pp.
Examine the effects of industrial settlement and urbanisation on the development of agriculture, markets and rural society.

61-2 BYERLEE, DEREK. Research on Migration in Africa: Past, Present and Future. Dept. of Agricultural Economics, Michigan State University, 1972, 32 pp.
Reports research carried out in Africa, including Tanzania and Kenya, reviewing critically trends in rural-urban migration, and suggesting directions for future research.

61-3 COLLIER, VALERIE C. and REMPEL, HENRY. 'The divergence of private from social costs in rural-urban migration: a case study of Nairobi, Kenya'. Mimeographed. IDS Disc P 181, Oct. 1973, 20 pp.

(COLLIER, VALERIE C. and REMPEL, HENRY)
Considers the determinants of private and social costs connected with urban unemployed and attempts to quantify the major private and social costs of migration to determine whether they diverge significantly.

61-4 ELKAN, WALTER. 'Circular migration and the growth of towns in East Africa'. International Labour Review, Dec. 1967, pp. 581-589.
Advocates measures to raise incomes in the rural economy to reduce the urban-rural differential incentive to migration.

61-5 ______. 'Is a proletariat emerging in Nairobi?' Mimeographed. IDS Disc P 168, 1973, 16 pp.
Argues that a substantial number in Nairobi depend permanently upon wage employment, while ties with their villages of origin have become severed.

61-6 GHAI, DHARAM P., ed. Portrait of a Minority: The Asians in East Africa. Oxford University Press, Nairobi, 1965, 227 pp.
Includes 'An Economic Survey' by Ghai, which sketches the main patterns of Asian economic activity in the post-war period and evaluates their role in economic development of East Africa.

61-7 GRAHAM, J. D. 'A case study of migrant labour in Tanzania'. African Studies Review, April 1970, pp. 23-33.
Discusses the impact on unskilled labourers of migration from Njombe district in the south to the sisal industry in the north-east.

61-8 HIRST, M. A. 'Net migration patterns over Tanzania'. East African Geographical Review, 1969, pp. 25-36.

61-9 JURGENS, H. W. An Investigation of Internal Migration in Tanzania. IFO, Munich, 1968, 166 pp.
Concludes that tribal movements will have a beneficial effect on the development of Tanzania.

61-10 Kenya, Central Bureau of Statistics. 'A preliminary report on the Kenya High and Middle Level Manpower Survey, 1972'. K Stat Dig, Dec. 1972, pp. 4-9.
Describes methods and summarises results, showing availability, nationality and distribution of high-level personnel.

POPULATION, MANPOWER

61-11 LE MELLE, W. J. 'The changing role of the planning adviser in East Africa'. African Review, June 1973, pp. 309-325.
Analyses pre- and post-independence uses of expatriate planning staff.

61-12 OMINDE, S. H. Land and Population Movement in Kenya. Northwestern University Press, Evanston, 1969, 204 pp.
Analyses the main currents of migration and their effects on resource use, employment and development.

61-13 RAY, ROBERT S. Labour Force Survey of Tanzania. Mimeographed. Ministry of Economic Affairs and Development Planning, Dar-es-Salaam, Jan. 1966, 156 pp.
Provides quantitative and qualitative benchmark data on major characteristics of labour supply, with commentary.

61-14 REMPEL, H. 'The rural-to-urban migrant in Kenya'. African Urban Notes, Spring, 1971, pp. 53-72.
Describes the background and personal characteristics of the men who moved to one of eight large centres in 1964-68.
See also essay with Todaro in Ominde and Ejiogu, entry 60-30.

61-15 SABOT, R. H. Education, Income Distribution and Rates of Urban Migration in Tanzania. Mimeographed. ERB, paper 72/6, Sept. 1972, 40 pp.
Describes how the labour market has responded to an increase in school-leavers and discusses the determinants of rural-urban migration.

61-16 SEMPEPBWA, E. K. K. 'Overseas sources of high level manpower'. EAJ, Aug. 1965, pp. 21-30.
Surveys post-independence technical assistance to Uganda.

61-17 TABER, S. R. 'Economic opportunity and urban orientation as factors in Uganda migration'. Geography Papers, 1969, pp. 29-42.

61-18 No entry.

61-19 TEMU, PETER E. 'The employment of foreign consultants in Tanzania: its value and limitations'. The African Review, 1973, No. 1, pp. 69-84.
Examines the qualitative and quantitative contributions of foreign consultants.

61-20 THOMAS, R. L. Manpower Development for Industrialisation, Country Case Study: United Republic of Tanzania. U.N. Centre for Industrial Development, New York, 1966.

61-21 TODARO, MICHAEL P. Education and Rural-Urban Migration: Theoretical Constructs and Empirical Evidence from Kenya. Mimeographed. Institute of Development Studies, University of Sussex, Sept. 1971, 34 pp.
Provides a framework for analysing the economic determinants of rural-urban migration and for ascertaining the impact of government policies to alleviate urban unemployment.
See also essay with Rempel in Ominde and Ejiogu (eds): entry 60-30.

62 - Productivity, incomes, industrial relations

62-1 AMSDEN, ALICE H. International Firms and Labour in Kenya, 1945-1970. Frank Cass, London, 1972, 208 pp.
Discusses international firms' influence on economic and political behaviour of labour in the third world, with Kenya as an example.

62-2 GHAI, DHARAM, P. 'Incomes policy in Kenya: need, criteria and machinery'. EAER, June 1968, pp. 19-34.
Argues that for equity and rapid expansion of employment, increases in wage rates should be slowed down to 4 per cent p.a., and profits controlled through fiscal and price policies.

62-3 _____. 'Strategy for a public sector wage policy in Kenya'. Mimeographed. IDS Disc P 65, May 1968, 11 pp.
Views the issues of wages and salaries in the public sector from the perspective of the national economy and social objectives. Urges the need for restraint in fixing public sector wage and salary levels.

62-4 GHAI, DHARAM P. and HOLLEN, CHARLES. 'The Industrial Court in Kenya: an economic analysis'. Mimeographed. IDS Disc P 73, Nov. 1968, 22 pp.
The Court was created to reduce the incidence of strikes by looking into the problems of wages and terms of service in the interests of both parties. Suggests ways in which it could be made more effective.

POPULATION, MANPOWER

62-5 HOUSE, WILLIAM J. 'Earnings per worker differentials in the provinces of Kenya, 1963-70'. J Dev Areas, April 1975.
Finds widening provincial differentials in 1963-67 and a narrowing in 1967-70. Seeks to explain these trends by reference to supply and demand conditions and differences in modern sector industrial structures.

62-6 _____. 'Wages, employment and productivity in Kenya: some further evidence'. EAER, June 1973, pp. 73-77.
Attempts to bring some further statistical evidence to bear on the relationship between wages and productivity changes in Kenya. Indicates that relationships between productivity and wage changes are consistent and relatively high.

62-7 HOUSE, WILLIAM J. and REMPEL, HENRY. 'The determinants of and changes in the structure of wages and employment in the manufacturing sector of the Kenya economy, 1967-1972'. Mimeographed. IDS Disc P 207, Dec. 1974, 31 pp.
Find considerable dispersion among industries in wages paid, which are explained by ability to pay, skilled labour required, and differences in the proportion of the labour force employed in Nairobi and in government enterprises.

62-8 International Labour Office. Report to the Government of the United Republic of Tanzania on Wages, Incomes and Price Policy. H. A. Turner, Chairman. Government Printer, Dar-es-Salaam, 1967, 45 pp.
Finds that past wage increases have simply shared out the same wage-bill among a smaller number of employees. Urges early action to control wages, prices and profits, and the creation of an Industrial Tribunal to supervise wage policy.

62-9 JACKSON, DUDLEY. 'Economic development and income distribution in Eastern Africa'. J Mod Afr Studs, Dec. 1971, pp. 531-542.
Shows that despite capital investment there has been little expansion in employment, and persisting income inequalities.

62-10 JOHNSON, G. E. 'The determination of individual hourly earnings in urban Kenya'. Mimeographed. IDS Disc P 115, Sept. 1971, 33 pp.
Investigates factors accounting for earnings differentials.

62-11 JOHNSON, G. E. and WHITELAW, W. E. 'Urban-rural income transfers in Kenya: an estimated remittances function'. Econ Dev Cult Change, April 1974, pp. 473-79.
Assesses the proportion of income remitted by urban wage earners to friends and relatives in rural areas.

62-12 Kenya, Republic of. The Policy on Trade Union Organisation in Kenya. Government Printer, Nairobi, 1965, 8 pp.
Presents the report of a Ministerial Committee recommending the creation of a Central Organisation of Trade Unions (COTU), and confirms the government's acceptance of this.

62-13 _____. Report of the Salaries Review Commission. H. Miller-Craig, Chairman. Government Printer, Nairobi, 1967, 138 pp.
Reviews and recommends changes in terms and conditions for all grades of the public service, to secure a stable administration.

62-14 KING, J. R. 'Wages, employment and productivity in Kenya: a comment'. EAER, June 1972, pp. 71-74.
Suggests that a high degree of agnosticism is still proper on the question of what effects a restrictive wage policy in Kenya would have on aggregate labour demand.

62-15 KNIGHT, J. B. 'Earnings, employment, education and income distribution in Uganda'. OIES Bull, Nov. 1968, pp. 267-297.
Analyses relationships between certain variables, and discusses the effects of wage behaviour on Uganda's development.

62-16 _____. Measuring Urban-rural Income Differentials. Mimeographed. Institute of Development Studies, University of Sussex, Sept. 1971, 33 pp.
Using material from Ghana, Uganda and Zambia, compares marginal supply price of labour from the rural sector and the marginal urban income of such migrants.

62-17 LARSEN, ARNE. Variation in Income Among Farming Areas in Sukumaland and Related Policy Implications. Mimeographed. ERB paper 70/6, 1970, 21 pp.
Investigates whether substantial inequalities exist among rural areas, isolates the factors responsible, and suggests means by which inequalities may be reduced.

62-18 MAPOLU, HENRY. 'The organisation and participation of workers in Tanzania'. The African Review, 1972, No. 3, pp. 381-416.

POPULATION, MANPOWER

(MAPOLU, HENRY)
Examines relationships between socio-economic systems and the theory and practice of workers' participation.

62-19 NWANUNOBI, ONYEKA C. 'Wage labour and the politics of Nigeria and Kenya: a comparative study'. African Studies Review, April 1974, pp. 77-104.
Compares activities of trade unions in Nigeria and Kenya.

62-20 PACK, HOWARD. 'Employment and productivity in Kenyan manufacturing'. EAER, Dec. 1972, pp. 29-52.
Argues 1) that there is considerable variation in feasible efficient production methods, particularly in peripheral operations; 2) substantial gains in labour productivity without capital deepening occur due to the gradual elimination of excess capacity.

62-21 SCOTT, ROGER D. The Determination of Statutory Minimum Wages in East Africa. Mimeographed. East African Institute of Social Research, Conference Proceedings, Jan. 1965, 12 pp.
Shows how decisions on national resource allocation are influenced by political, social and economic pressures.

62-22 _____. The Development of Trade Unions in Uganda. East African Publishing House, Nairobi, 1966, 200 pp.
Emphasises that lack of long-term interest in wage employment impeded the development of trade unions, with most workers resuming tenure of tribal land after a short spell of wage employment.

62-23 SENGA, W. M. 'Wages, market imperfections and labour absorption in Kenya manufacturing industries'. EAER, June 1973, pp. 53-72.
Argues that doing away with minimum wages or holding down wages in an industrial sector with foreign investment-induced market imperfections is not likely to lead to higher labour absorption.

62-24 SINGH, MAKHAN. 'The East African Trades Union Congress, 1949-50: the first central organisation of trade unions in Kenya'. Hadith, No. 4, 1972, pp. 233-49.
A largely descriptive account of its formation and activities.

62-25 TORDOFF, WILLIAM. 'Trade unionism in Tanzania'. J Dev Studs, July 1966, pp. 408-430.
Examines trade union-government relationships in Tanzania.

62-26 WHEELER, MARK. 'Professional fees in the Kenya building industry'. Mimeographed. IDS Disc P 60, Jan. 1968, 30 pp.
The scale structure of fees for professional designers is determined by construction costs, bringing automatic rises in design costs per unit. Urges that proposals be drawn up for discussion with professionals.

63 - Employment and unemployment; labour-intensity, the choice of techniques

63-1 BARYARUHA, AZARIAS. Factors Affecting Industrial Employment: A Study of Ugandan Experience, 1954 to 1964. Oxford University Press, London, 1967, 83 pp.
Investigates employers' attitudes towards the substitution and training of labour.

63-2 BYERLEE, DEREK and EICHER, CARL. Rural Employment, Migration and Economic Development. Dept. of Agricultural Economics, Michigan State University, 1972, 47 pp.
Reports research carried out in Africa, including material on Kenya and Tanzania.

63-3 DAVIES, DAVID G. 'A critical discussion of ILO report on employment in Kenya'. Pakistan Development Review, Autumn 1973, pp. 283-92.
A review article.
See entry 63-15.

63-4 ELKAN, WALTER. 'Urban unemployment in East Africa'. International Affairs, July 1970, pp. 517-528.
Examines employment trends in Kenya and Uganda. Argues that the stagnation of employment is not inevitable but may be the result of policy decisions or lack of policy.

63-5 EMMERIJ, LOUIS. 'A new look at some strategies for increasing productive employment in Africa'. International Labour Review, Sept. 1974, pp. 199-218.
Reports the chief points and conclusions to emerge from a 1973 Policy Seminar on the ILO Report on Kenya.
See also entry 63-15.

63-6 GHAI, DHARAM P. 'Employment performance, prospects and policies in Kenya'. EAJ, Nov. 1970, pp. 4-11.
An analysis of past trends and future prospects for employment, and an evaluation of policies adopted or proposed to deal with unemployment.

POPULATION, MANPOWER

63-7 GUTKIND, P. C. W. 'The energy of despair: social organisation of the unemployed in 2 African cities: Lagos and Nairobi'. Civilisation, 1967, pp. 380-405.

63-8 GWYER, G. D. 'Trends in Kenyan agriculture in relation to employment'. J Mod Afr Studs, Sept. 1973, pp. 393-403.
Discusses the unemployment problem in Kenya through an analysis of trends in employment in both large- and small-scale agriculture.

63-9 HARRIS, J. R. and TODARO, M. P. 'Urban unemployment in East Africa: an economic analysis of policy alternatives'. EAER, Dec. 1968, pp. 17-36.
Argue that unless the interrelationships between rural-urban earnings differentials, job creation, and migration are fully appreciated, policies directed towards one aspect of the problem will make a minimal impact on urban unemployment.

63-10 _____. 'Wages, industrial employment and labour productivity in a developing economy: the Kenyan experience'. EAER, June 1969, pp. 29-46.
Argue that wage movements, especially for unskilled African labourers, play a significant role in influencing entrepreneurial employment decisions.

63-11 HENLEY, JOHN S. 'Employment relationships and economic development--the Kenyan experience'. J Mod Afr Studs, Dec. 1973, pp. 559-589.
Some aspects of the development of the Kenyan labour market in pre- and post-independence periods.

63-12 HENNING, PETER H. and HOUSE, WILLIAM J. 'The problem of slow employment growth in the manufacturing sector of less developed economies: some preliminary observations from the Kenya experience'. Journal of Eastern Africa Research and Development, 1975, No. 2.
Conclude that the indiscriminate promotion of small-scale modern sector plants may contribute little to employment creation because many of them use less labour per unit of output than larger plants in the same industry.

63-13 HUTTON, CAROLINE. Reluctant Farmers? East African Publishing House, Nairobi, 1973, 331 pp.
A study of unemployment and planned rural development in Uganda.

63-14 _____. 'Unemployment in Kampala and Jinja, Uganda'. Canadian Journal of African Studies, Spring 1970, pp. 431-440.
Because of the seasonality of cash crops, concludes that peaks of urban unemployment will continue to manifest themselves.

63-15 International Labour Office. Employment, Incomes and Equality: A Strategy for Increasing Productive Employment in Kenya. Geneva, 1972, 600 pp.
A seminal report based on the findings of an inter-agency mission to Kenya under the World Employment Programme. Includes thirty-one technical papers prepared for the mission. Proposes a strategy of redistribution from growth.

63-16 _____. Employment in Africa: Some Critical Issues. Geneva, 1973, 285 pp.
Includes Singer, Hans and Jolly, Richard 'Unemployment in an African setting: lessons of the employment strategy mission to Kenya'; Elkan, Walter 'Out of school education and training for primary school leavers in rural Kenya: a proposal'.
See also entry 63-15.

63-17 Kenya, Central Bureau of Statistics. 'The enumeration of employees, 1964'. K Stat Dig, June 1965, pp. 1-4.
Provisional results on employment and earnings for 1963 and 1964.

63-18 Kenya, National Assembly. Report of the Select Committee on Unemployment. Government Printer, Nairobi, Dec. 1970, 59 pp.
Examines unemployment in Kenya, and recommends measures to alleviate it.

63-19 Kenya, Republic of. Sessional Paper on Employment. Government Printer, Nairobi, May 1973, 73 pp.
The official response to the ILO report on Kenya, setting out the government's policy proposals.
See also entry no. 63-15.

63-20 LEYS, COLIN. 'Interpreting African underdevelopment: reflections on the ILO report on employment, incomes and equality in Kenya'. African Affairs, Oct. 1973, pp. 419-29.
Criticises the ILO Report (63-15) as politically naive in its treatment of the informal sector and in its policy recommendations.

POPULATION, MANPOWER

63-21 LIVINGSTONE, IAN. 'Creating employment in Kenya'. J Admin Overseas, April 1974, pp. 374-382.
A review article of the ILO Kenya report.
See entry 63-15.

63-22 McFARQUHAR, A. M. M. and EVANS, G. B. ANEURYN. Employment Creation in Primary Production. OECD Development Centre, Paris, 1972, 163 pp.
Case studies of employment potential in the coffee industries of Brazil and Kenya.

63-23 MAITHA, J. K. 'Capital-labour substitution in manufacturing in a developing economy: the case of Kenya'. EAER, Dec. 1973, pp. 43-52.
Finds a significant relationship between factor proportions and factor prices, with elasticities of substitution significantly greater than zero.

63-24 _____. 'A short-term employment function for Kenyan manufacturing'. EAER, Dec. 1972, pp. 67-72.
Argues that the level of employment in manufacturing is in equilibrium, or very close to it, and therefore to increase employment substantially some structural shifts must occur.

63-25 MUREITHI, LEOPOLD P. 'Demographic and technological variables in Kenya's employment scene'. EAER, 1974, No. 1, pp. 27-43.
Presents and applies a labour-absorption model of production, and concludes that capital-intensity has been increasing.

63-26 NIGAM, S. B. L. and SINGER, H. W. 'Labour turnover and employment: some evidence from Kenya'. International Labour Review, Dec. 1974, pp. 479-493.
Authors believe that changes in labour turnover may be more important for job prospects than changes in the overall rate of employment.

63-27 OKAI, MATTHEW. 'Some aspects of agricultural labour use in the main short grass zone of Uganda'. EAJ Rural Devel, 1972, Nos. 1 and 2, pp. 103-122.
A study of labour use in peasant agriculture in Eastern and Northern Uganda.

63-28 RADO, EMIL R. 'Employment, incomes policy: Kenya's new development plan'. EAJ, March 1970, pp. 13-20.
A statistical illustration of the unemployment problems faced by the Kenyan planners.

63-29 SHEFFIELD, JAMES R., ed. Education, Employment and Rural Development. East African Publishing House, Nairobi, 1967, 499 pp.
The proceedings of a conference held at Kericho, Kenya, 1966; comprising collection of articles and an introductory chapter summarising the conclusions of the conference.

63-30 SINGER, H. and JOLLY, R. 'Unemployment in an African setting: Lessons of the employment mission to Kenya'. International Labour Review, Feb. 1973, pp. 103-115.
Discuss factors which underlie Kenya's employment problems and strategies to alleviate it.
See also entry 63-15.

63-31 WALLACE, TINA. 'Working in rural Buganda: a study of the occupational activities of young people in rural villages'. The African Review, 1973, No. 1, pp. 133-178.
Defines a theoretical approach to the problem of employment and uses it to analyse employment experiences in a Bugandan village.

63-32 WEEKS, SHELDON G. 'Where are all the jobs? The informal sector in Bugisu, Uganda'. The African Review, 1973, No. 1, pp. 111-132.
Describes the range of informal activities that are open to, and utilised by, rural youths.

63-33 WERLIN, H. H. 'The informal sector: the implications of the ILO's study of Kenya'. African Studies Review, April 1974, pp. 205-213.
Questions whether proposals for helping hawkers and squatters are likely to be accepted.

64 - Manpower and educational planning; Africanisation

64-1 ALDINGTON, T. J. et al. 'The economics of Kenyanization: some professional comments and recommendations'. EAJ, 1968, pp. 21-29.
Discusses the policy of Kenyanization of private commerce and industry.

64-2 ANDERSON, C. ARNOLD and FOSTER, J. PHILIP. 'Potentials for federation of East African educational programmes'. J Dev Studs, Oct. 1966, pp. 59-81.
The socio-political and economic aspects of integrated educational planning in East Africa.

POPULATION, MANPOWER

64-3 ANDERSON, J. E. 'The Kenya Education Commission Report 1964: An African view of educational planning'. Comparative Education Review, June 1965, pp. 201-7.
Surveys educational resources and problems, with recommendations.

64-4 BARBER, WILLIAM J. 'Some questions about labour force analysis in agrarian economies, with particular reference to Kenya'. EAER, June 1966, pp. 23-37.
Argues that standard macro-economic employment analyses are not very helpful in economies such as Kenya and presents an alternative stressing labour input and output relationships.

64-5 BIENEFELD, M. A. Manpower Planning and the University: The Position in Education, Arts, and Social Sciences. Mimeographed. ERB Paper 70/2, 1970, 32 pp.
Summarizes the University of Dar-es-Salaam's performance to 1969/70 vis-a-vis manpower plans.

64-6 _____. 'Planning people'. Development and Change, 1972/73, No. 1, pp. 51-77.
A discussion of Tanzania's attempt to plan training, allocation and remuneration of its manpower consistent with its overall commitment to a socialist development path.

64-7 BROWNSTEIN, L. Education and Development in Rural Kenya: A Case Study of Primary School Graduates. Praeger, New York, 1972, 212 pp.
Examines Kenya's educational system and recommends a new strategy paying more attention to the output of the primary schools.

64-8 BUCKNAIL, J. J. 'Government policies and programmes for increasing African participation and efficiency in the distributive sector of the Kenyan economy with major reference to the Kenya National Trading Corporation'. African Urban Notes, Fall 1970, pp. 24-34.
A short survey.

64-9 CASTLE, E. B. Growing up in East Africa. Oxford University Press, London, 1966, 272 pp.
Part III includes 'Educational Resources and Manpower Needs'. Reviews current educational planning, suggesting lines of development for all parts of the educational system.

64-10 CHESSWAS, J. D. Educational Planning and Development in Uganda. Unesco, Paris, 1966, 97 pp.
Suggests the structure of an educational planning unit and how it might best be fitted into the institutional framework of national development.

64-11 GAVIN, ROBERT. 'Correcting racial imbalance in employment in Kenya'. International Labour Review, Jan.-Feb. 1967, pp. 61-77.
Examines employment measures taken to promote racial balance and Africanisation.

64-12 HARBISON, FREDERICK H. and MYERS, CHARLES A. Manpower and Education: Country Studies in Economic Development. McGraw-Hill, New York, 1965, 343 pp.
Country studies of the processes of human resource development and their relationship to economic growth. Includes Thomas, Robert L. 'High level manpower in the economic development of Uganda'; Hunter, Guy. 'Issues in manpower policy: some contrasts from East Africa and Southeast Asia'.

64-13 HUNTER, GUY. 'Manpower, employment and education in the rural economy of Tanzania'. Educational Development in Africa; III. Integration and Administration. UNESCO, Paris, 1969, pp. 83-118.
Examines employment opportunities for those with little or no education, and discusses the problems of relating educational and manpower planning.

64-14 JOLLY, RICHARD. Planning Education for African Development. East African Publishing House, Nairobi, 1969, 168 pp.
Develops the concept of 'age-education profiles' to show levels of educational attainment and how it is built up through the educational system. Includes a chapter on educational expansion in Uganda.

64-15 No Entry.

64-16 Kenya, Republic of. High-level Manpower Requirements and Resources in Kenya, 1964-1970. Government Printer, Nairobi, 1965, 46 pp.
Covers estimates of manpower supply, demand-supply relationships, agricultural employment and the problems of Africanisation.

64-17 _____. Kenyanisation of Personnel in the Private Sector. Government Printer, Nairobi, 1967, 4 pp.

POPULATION, MANPOWER

(Kenya, Republic of)
A statement of policy relating to the employment of non-citizens.

64-18 MWINGIRA, AUGUSTIN C. and PRATT, SIMON. The Process of Educational Planning in Tanzania. UNESCO, Paris, 1967, 102 pp.
Stresses the need for constant co-operation and negotiation among units of government; and the role of educational innovation and reform.

64-19 RADO, EMIL R. 'Manpower planning in East Africa'. EAER, June 1967, pp. 1-30.
A survey of factors affecting manpower, strategies to alleviate the problems, and difficulties encountered in this exercise.

64-20 _____. 'The 1966-71 Uganda manpower plan: a note'. J Dev Studs, 1967, pp. 451-456.
Examines the relationship between total output and the structure of high-level employment.

64-21 RADO, E. R. and JOLLY, R. 'The demand for manpower--an East African case study'. J Dev Studs, April 1965, pp. 226-250.
Discuss two bases upon which to calculate future manpower requirements.

64-22 RESNICK, I. N. 'Manpower development in Tanzania'. J Mod Afr Studs, May 1967, pp. 107-124.
Indicates the dimensions and problems of manpower planning, and attempts to solve them.

64-23 SKOROV, GEORGE. Integration of Educational and Economic Planning in Tanzania. UNESCO, Paris, 1966, 79 pp.
Discusses problems in educational planning and the need for an educational system to fit development priorities.

64-24 SMYTH, JOHN. 'The political economy of educational planning in Uganda'. Comparative Education Review, Oct. 1970, pp. 350-362.
Presents a history and critique of educational planning in Uganda since 1940.

64-25 THIAS, HANS HEINRICH and CARNOY, MARTIN. Cost-benefit Analysis in Education: A Case Study of Kenya. World Bank Staff Occasional Paper No. 14, Johns Hopkins Press, Baltimore, 1972, 193 pp.

(THIAS, HANS HEINRICH and CARNOY, MARTIN)
Provide comparative rates of return for investments within education and outside; provide manpower projections which are sensitive to future changes in wage differentials. Argue the superiority of a cost-benefit approach over the manpower requirements approach to educational planning. See also articles by Carnoy and Thias in EAER, Dec. 1971 and April 1972.

64-26 TOBIN, JAMES. 'Notes on the economic theory of expulsion and expropriation'. J Dev Studs, June 1974, pp. 7-18
A theoretical analysis of issues raised by Africanisation in East Africa.

64-27 Uganda, Ministry of Commerce and Industry. Report of the Committee on Africanisation of Commerce and Industry in Uganda. Francis X. Mugeni, Chairman. Government Printer, Entebbe, 1968, 52 pp.
Presents a comprehensive programme of Africanisation, including top executive posts in public and private companies.

64-28 Uganda, Ministry of Planning and Economic Development. High Level Manpower Survey, 1967; And Analysis of Requirements, 1967-1981. Nicholas Bennet, Director. Government Printer, Entebbe, 1967, 53 pp.
Presents survey results, methods adopted, projections and recommendations on Ugandanisation.

7 - SOCIAL ECONOMICS

70 - Economics of education

70-1 Adult Education, Board of. Adult Education in Nation Building. Adult Education Secretariat, Nairobi, 1973, 193 pp.
Papers presented at a conference in July 1973. Contributions include papers on education and training for agriculture, co-operatives, health and small businesses.

70-2 ANDERSON, JOHN E. The Struggle for the School: The Interaction of Missionary, Colonial Government, and Nationalist Enterprise in the Development of Formal Education in Kenya. Longmans, London, 1970, 192 pp.
An account of the historical development of education in Kenya which relates current educational problems to previously developed patterns.

SOCIAL ECONOMICS

70-3 CHÂU, TA NGOC, et al. Population Growth and Costs of Education in Developing Countries. UNESCO International Institute for Educational Planning, Paris, 1972, 313 pp.
Includes Châu, Ta Ngoc and Caillodes, Françoise 'Tanzania: A case study'.

70-4 CHEGE, F. and ERGAS, Z. 'Primary school education in Kenya: An attempt at evaluation'. Journal of Eastern African Research and Development, 1973, No. 2, pp. 95-111.
A critical examination of the growing inequities in the primary school system.

70-5 COURT, DAVID. 'The experience of higher education in East Africa: prospects for a developmental role' Mimeographed. IDS Disc P 216, Feb. 1975.
Looking particularly closely at the University of Dar-es-Salaam, attempts to assess prospects, and identify the growth points towards a new kind of development of East African universities.

70-6 COURT, DAVID and GHAI, DHARAM P., eds. Education, Society and Development: New Perspectives from Kenya. Oxford University Press, Nairobi, 1974, 345 pp.
A collection of papers on the structure and culture of Kenyan education; training, recruitment and employment; issues of equality; and alternatives in Kenyan education.

70-7 COWAN, L. G. The Cost of Learning: The Politics of Primary Education in Kenya. Columbia Teacher's College Press, New York, 1970, 106 pp.
Describes tensions between central and local administrative authorities since independence and provides information on the financing of primary education.

70-8 CURRIE, J. and MAAS, I. L. 'Uganda's secondary school graduates: postponement of labour market entry'. Manpower and Unemployment Research in Africa, April 1974, pp. 14-31.
Results of a survey of 1971 final-year students.

70-9 FIELDS, GARY S. 'The educational system of Kenya: an economist's view.' Mimeographed. IDS Disc P 103, April 1971, 47 pp.
Basic data on the economics of education, intended to supplement a 1966 area handbook for Kenya.

70-10 FORD, R. J. C. 'The village polytechnic programme in Kenya'. International Labour Review, April 1975, pp. 307-320.

70-11 GODFREY, MARTIN. 'Training and the employment problem: some reflections based on Kenya's experience'. Manpower and Unemployment Research in Africa, April 1974, pp. 60-68.
Discusses the merits of formal and nonformal methods of training; praises the Village Polytechnic programme.

70-12 GODFREY, MARTIN and MUTISO, G. C. M. 'The political economy of self-help: Kenya's "Harambee" Institutes of Technology'. Canadian Journal of African Studies, 1974, No. 1, pp. 109-133.
Describes the campaign to establish the institutes, and their possible economic and social effects.

70-13 HALL, B. L. and REMTULLA, K., eds. Adult Education and National Development. East African Literature Bureau, Nairobi, 1973, 128 pp.
Includes Mwakotobe, R. Y. 'The role of correspondence education in co-operative training in Tanzania'; Albinson, F. and Kassam, Y. 'Training of adult educators in Tanzania'.

70-14 HEIJNEN, J. D. Development and Education in the Mwanza District (Tanzania): A Case Study of Migration and Peasant Farming. Bronder-Offset, Rotterdam, 1968, 171 pp.
Argues that primary education should disseminate knowledge which will help children become progressive farmers.

70-15 HUNTER, GUY. Education for a Developing Region: A Study in East Africa. Allen and Unwin, London, 1963, 119 pp.
Appraises educational opportunities and problems in East Africa.

70-16 JOLLY, RICHARD, ed. Education in Africa. East Africa Publishing House, Nairobi, 1969, 313 pp.
Papers on East Africa presented at a September 1968 conference. Topics covered include an analysis of enrolments and costs; educational policies in Tanzania and Kenya; occupational attitudes of Ugandan school leavers; and rural and adult education.

70-17 JOLLY, RICHARD and RADO, E. Education in Uganda: Reflections on the Report of the Uganda Education Committee. Mimeographed. East African Institute of Social Research Conference Proceedings, 1964, pp. 69-79.
Examines the content and structure of education, its improvement and adaptation to the needs of the country.

SOCIAL ECONOMICS

70-18 KAJUBI, W. S. 'New directions in teacher education in East Africa'. International Review of Education, 1971, pp. 197-210.
Concludes that education at all levels, especially in the primary school, should be made more practical and agriculturally oriented.

70-19 KAMOGA, K. FRED. Wastage among Teachers in Buganda. Mimeographed. East African Institute of Social Research, Kampala, Dec. 1963, 17 pp.
General discussion of the problems of the teaching profession and their effects on the economy.

70-20 Kenya, Republic of. Education Committee Report. 2 parts. S. H. Ominde, Chairman. Nairobi, Dec. 1964; July 1965, pp. 166; 63.
Part I contains a comprehensive review of education in Kenya and deals with questions of policy. Part II discusses the quantitative aspects of education in the light of a manpower survey.

70-21 _____. Report of the Agricultural Education Commission. J. R. Weir, Chairman. Government Printer, Nairobi, 1967, 211 pp.
Examines the existing provisions for agricultural education and proposes a plan to improve the supply of suitably trained manpower.

70-22 KINYANJUI, KABIRU. 'The distribution of education resources and opportunities in Kenya'. Mimeographed. IDS Disc P 208, Aug. 1974, 41 pp.
A preliminary analysis, concluding that educational benefits are being distributed in favour of the economically powerful districts and provinces in Kenya.

70-23 _____. 'Education, training and employment of secondary school leavers in Kenya'. Education in Eastern Africa, 1971, No. 1, pp. 3-21.
Presents data collected from a sample of school leavers who completed Form IV in 1965-68.

70-24 _____. 'Opportunities for school leavers outside the major towns of Kenya'. Mimeographed. IDS Disc P 188, July 1974, 13 pp.
Points out that most secondary school leavers are attracted to the major towns, where most of the opportunities for wage employment exist.

70-25 KIPKORIR, B. E. 'Non-formal education in Kenya'. Mimeographed. IDS Disc P 211, Dec. 1974, 30 pp.
Describes and evaluates selected programmes of non-formal education, dividing them into three main categories.

70-26 KNIGHT, J. B. The Costing and Financing of Educational Development in Tanzania. UNESCO, Louvain, 1966, 80 pp.

70-27 MAXWELL, ROBERT. 'Occupational inclinations and attitudes towards rural modernisation of students in selected Kenyan secondary schools'. EAJ Rural Devel, 1969, No. 2, pp. 61-74.
The paper reports the responses from male students in Kenyan secondary schools in regard to accepting certain occupations.

70-28 MERINAR, C. CALVIN. 'Design and operation of the veterinary training institute small-holder dairy unit--an example of intensive dairy farming in Uganda'. EAJ Rural Devel, 1973, Nos. 1 and 2, pp. 165-178.
Economic evaluation of practical training facilities in animal husbandry and pasture agronomy.

70-29 MORIS, J. R. The Impact of Secondary Education upon Student Attitudes towards Agriculture: Some Preliminary Considerations. Mimeographed. East African Institute of Social Research Conference Proceedings Part D, Jan. 1966, 28 pp.
Analyses negative student attitudes towards agriculture and suggests changes in syllabus so as to attract students into agriculture.

70-30 O'CONNOR, E. 'Contrasts in educational development in Kenya and Tanzania'. African Affairs, Jan. 1974, pp. 67-84.
Argues that despite different approaches there has been little change in the structure of education in either country since independence.

70-31 ODIA, SOLOMON. 'Rural education and training in Tanzania'. International Labour Review, Jan. 1971, pp. 13-28.
Summarises the elements of Tanzania's production-oriented education and training system, and how it is linked to development goals.

70-32 PROSSER, ROY. Adult Education for Developing Countries. East African Publishing House, Nairobi, 1967, 151 pp.
Covers the relationship between adult education and national development, its organisation and planning, and its content and method.

SOCIAL ECONOMICS

70-33 RADO, E. R.; MORGAN, JAMES; and SHEPARD, DON. 'The selection of form four leavers for further education, training and employment'. Mimeographed. IDS Disc P 94, June 1970, 18 pp.
Investigate what has happened to Form 4 school leavers since 1965 and what proportion proceed to further education.

70-34 RAJU, BEULAH M. Education in Kenya. Heinemann, London, 1973, 133 pp.
Analyses problems and perspectives in educational planning and administration.

70-35 ROGERS, DANIEL C. 'Student loan programmes and the returns to investment in higher levels of education in Kenya'. Econ Dev Cult Change, Jan. 1972, pp. 243-259.
Investigates private rates of return to higher-level education in Kenya, and the feasibility of a student loan programme.

70-36 SOMERSET, H. C. A. 'Educational research in Kenya: a personal viewpoint'. Mimeographed. IDS Disc P 97, Oct. 1970, 12 pp.
Suggests priorities for educational research in Kenya.

70-37 STABLER, E. Education since Uhuru: The Schools of Kenya. Wesleyan University Press, Middletown, 1969, 179 pp.
Concludes that education in Kenya will have to broaden its academic base to contribute significantly to rural development.

*70-38 Uganda, Government of. A Cost/Benefit Evaluation of Education to School Certificate and Graduate Level. Government Printer, Entebbe, 1963.

*70-39 Uganda, Ministry of Education. The Report of the Working Party on Secondary School Costs. Kampala, 1964.

70-40 Uganda, Republic of. Education in Uganda. E. B. Castle, Chairman. Government Printer, Kampala, 1963, 92 pp.
The report of a commission examining the content and structure of education, its improvement and adaptation to the needs of the country.

70-41 U.N. Food and Agriculture Organisation. Report to the Government of Kenya on Dairy Training. K. K. Hansen, Chairman. Rome, 1974, 22 pp.
Survey carried out to investigate extending practical dairy training at Egerton College. Emphasises that more people should be trained for the milk processing industry.

70-42 WILSON, D. N. Economic Aspects of Development Education Applied to East Africa. Syracuse University, New York, Jan. 1964, 39 pp.
Criticises the present educational system's failure to produce technicians and extension workers, and suggests educational innovations.

70-43 ZANOLI, NOA VERA. Education towards Development in Tanzania. Pharos-Verlag, Basel, 1971, 386 pp.
Results of a 1968 survey in Ulanga district, offering an anthropological analysis of the educational situation and recommendations for the implementation of a strategy of education for self-reliance.

71 - Health, housing, water, social policy

71-1 BIENEFELD, M. A. and BINHAMMER, H. H. Tanzanian Housing Finance and Housing Policy. Mimeographed. ERB, 1969, 26 pp.
Discuss the difficulties of providing housing finance and trace the development of housing policy since independence.

71-2 BINHAMMER, H. H. Financing Housing in Tanzania. ERB, 1969, 15 pp.
Surveys the growth and policies of institutions which provide finance for housing.

71-3 BLOOMBERG, L. N. and ABRAMS, C. United Nations Mission to Kenya on Housing. U.N. Dept. of Social and Economic Affairs, Government Printer, Nairobi, 1964, 79 pp.
Studies short- and long-term housing needs and makes policy recommendations.

71-4 CARRUTHERS, I. D. 'Assessing the contribution of rural water investment to development'. EAJ Rural Devel, 1970, No. 2, pp. 96-110.
Discusses the issues raised by the application of cost-benefit analysis to an expanded programme of rural water supplies in Kenya.
See also IDS Disc P 88, 1969, and IDS Working P 31, 1972.

71-5 _____. Impact and Economics of Community Water Supply. School of Rural Economics, Wye College, Ashford, Kent, 1973, 120 pp.
Documents experience and discusses problems related to rural water development in Kenya.

SOCIAL ECONOMICS

71-6 CARRUTHERS, I. D. 'A new approach to domestic water rating'. EAER, Dec. 1972, pp. 73-96.
A number of alternative rating strategies are feasible but if there is to be widespread adoption of piped water supplies, subsidies will be required.

71-7 ELKAN, WALTER. 'Some social policy implications of industrial development in East Africa'. International Social Science Journal, 1964, pp. 390-399.

71-8 GERSHENBERG, IRVING and HASKELL, MARK A. 'The distribution of medical services in Uganda'. Social Science and Medicine, 1972, pp. 353-72.
Studies the allocation of resources within the health service in the light of the objective of making medical services available to the greatest number of people in the shortest possible time.

71-9 GISH, OSCAR. 'Resource allocation, equality of access and health'. World Development, Dec. 1973, pp. 37-44.
Draws upon Tanzanian experiences to relate resource allocation in the health sector to the output of health, by contrasting access to, and utilisation of, available health services by urban and rural populations.

71-10 HARRIS, JOHN R. 'Some thoughts on a housing policy for Nairobi'. Mimeographed. IDS Disc P 78, April 1969, 15 pp.
Argues that the Nairobi housing problem is mainly the result of too few housing units for very low-income persons. Suggests criteria for future policies.

71-11 Kenya, Central Bureau of Statistics. 'Building cost index'. K Stat Dig, Sept. 1974, pp. 5-9.
Presents the methods used to estimate the cost of materials and labour to derive indices of construction costs of residential and non-residential buildings.

71-12 Kenya, Republic of. Housing Policy for Kenya. Government Printer, Nairobi, 1966, 8 pp.
Government observations on the report of U.N. Mission on Housing in Kenya.
See also entry No. 71-3.

71-13 _____. Report Made to the Minister for Commerce and Industry by the Working Party on Rent Control. S. N. Waruhui, Chairman. Government Printer, Nairobi, 1963, 17 pp.

(Kenya, Republic of)
Considers the desirability of legislation to impose controls on the rents of business premises, to benefit small traders.

71-14 _____. Report of the Committee of Inquiry into Rent Restriction Legislation. J. L. N. Konchellah, Chairman. Government Printer, Nairobi, 1963, 7 pp.
Recommends that all residential premises whose standard rent is £20 or more per month should be controlled.

71-15 MECK, MARGARETE. Problems and Prospects of Social Services in Kenya. Weltforum Verlag, Munich, 1971, 209 pp.
Discusses the development of social services, especially education and health.

71-16 TEMPLE, NELLE W. 'Housing preferences and policy in Kibera, Nairobi'. Mimeographed. IDS Disc P 196, March 1974, 47 pp.
Reviews the human impact of redevelopment at Kibera, concluding that more poor people are likely to be ill-housed after redevelopment than before. Makes policy recommendations.

71-17 TRIBE, M. A., ed. Housing in Uganda. Milton Obote Foundation, Kampala, 1969, 150 pp.

71-18 TRIBE, M. A. 'Patterns of urban housing demand in Uganda'. EAER, June 1968, pp. 35-50.
Shows factors affecting demand, i.e. ability and willingness to pay, geographical location and household size, and argues that the pattern has not changed for a long time.

71-19 Uganda, Government of. Report on the Setting up of a Contributory Social Security Scheme with Particular Reference to Persons in their Old Age. Government Printer, Entebbe, 1964.

71-20 VAN ZWANENBERG, ROGER. 'History and theory of urban poverty in Nairobi: the problems of slum development'. Mimeographed. IDS Disc P 139, 1972, 50 pp.
Attempts to explain the generation of poverty in Nairobi. Concludes that the problem is due to urban population growth too rapid for available housing, and wages too low to meet high housing costs.

SOCIAL ECONOMICS

71-21 WARNER, DENNIS. 'Formulating guidelines for rural water investment: the case of Tanzania'. EAJ Rural Devel, 1971, No. 1, pp. 69-91.
Sets out the necessary features of a planned approach to rural water projects.

71-22 WHITE, GILBERT; BRADLEY, DAVID, and WHITE, ANNE. Drawers of Water--Domestic Water Use in East Africa. University of Chicago Press, 1972, 306 pp.
Studies household water consumption and the economic and social costs of transporting it to the home.

72 - Regional and urban planning and policies

72-1 BERRY, L. et al. Some Aspects of Regional Planning in Tanzania. Bureau of Resource Assessment and Land Use Planning, University of Dar-es-Salaam, 1971, 46 pp.
Examine the types of plans implemented at different scales and suggest guidelines for their preparation in the future.

72-2 CHAMBERS, R. Some Background to Proposals for Development Plan Implementation at Provincial and Lower Levels in Kenya. Mimeographed. East African Institute of Social Research Conference Papers, Kampala, Jan. 1966, 15 pp.
Outlines the ideas of planning and some aspects of the social, economic, and organisational context out of which they arise; criticises certain proposals for plan implementation.

72-3 No entry.

72-4 FAIR, T. J. D. 'A regional approach to economic development in Kenya'. South African Geographic Journal, 1963, pp. 55-77.

72-5 FINUCANE, J. R. 'Hierarchy and participation in development: a case study of regional administration in Tanzania'. The African Review, 1972, No. 4, pp. 573-598.
Analysis of an administrative role-set in one of Tanzania's regions.

72-6 GAPPERT, GARRY. Regional Development and Economic Planning (2 papers). Afrika-Studiecentrum, Leiden, Dec. 1970, 28 pp., 21 pp.
Paper I discusses problems in regional development and economic planning. Paper II compares national and local policy towards implementation of village settlements, using cost-benefit analysis.

72-7 HUTTON, JOHN, ed. Urban Challenge in East Africa. East African Publishing House, Nairobi, 1972, 285 pp.
Collection of papers which focus on urban growth, planning and social development.

72-8 KIMANI, S. M. and TAYLOR, D. R. F. Growth Centres and Rural Development in Kenya. Maxim Printers, Thika (Kenya), 1973, 100 pp.
A study carried out in Muranga District. Urges that a spatial strategy for rural development be made more central in Kenya's development planning.

72-9 LAWRENCE, P. R.; RAIKES, P. L.; SAYLOR, R. G.; and WARNER, D. 'Regional planning in Tanzania: some institutional problems'. EAJ Rural Devel, 1974, Nos. 1 and 2, pp. 10-45.
Comment on issues affecting regional planning procedures and ways in which they could be improved.

72-10 LUTTRELL, WILLIAM L. 'Location planning and regional development in Tanzania'. Development and Change, 1972/73, No. 1, pp. 17-38.
Planning techniques and implementation mechanisms in rural Tanzania.

72-11 MASCARENHAS, ADOLF C. 'Factors influencing Tanzania's urban policy'. African Urban Notes, Fall 1972, pp. 24-42.
Analyses urban policies in the five-year plans and speculates on the possible effects of decentralisation.

72-12 OBUDHO, R. A. Urbanisation and Regional Planning in Western Kenya. Mimeographed. African Studies Association, Philadelphia, Nov. 1972, 43 pp.
Emphasises co-ordinated national, urban, and regional planning to provide basic services for hinterland markets surrounding growth centres.

72-13 OGENDO, REUBEN B. 'The significance of industrial zoning to rural industrial development in Kenya: a study of the facts and methodology'. Cahiers d'Etudes Africaines, Paris, 1967, pp. 444-484.
Argues that decentralisation of manufacturing industries will employ idle resources in the rural sector.

72-14 SAFIER, M., ed. The Role of Urban and Regional Planning in National Development for East Africa. Milton Obote Foundation, Kampala, 1970, 299 pp.

(SAFIER, M.)
A collection of papers arranged under the headings, National and Regional Planning Perspectives; Industrial and Urban Growth; The Urban Planning Perspective; Rural Development.

72-15 SAFIER, M. and LANGLANDS, B. W., eds. Perspectives on Urban Planning for Uganda. Institute of Social Research, Kampala, 1969, 238 pp.
Collection of papers arranged under following headings: 1) On plans and planning; 2) On the foundations; 3) On design and society; 4) Evaluation and education.

72-16 SAYLOR, R. G. and LIVINGSTONE, I. 'Regional planning in Tanzania'. African Review, Sept. 1971, pp. 53-75.
Investigates the prospects and problems of decentralisation in planning.

72-17 TAYLOR, D. R. F. 'The role of the smaller urban place in development: a case study from Kenya'. African Urban Notes, Fall 1972, pp. 7-23.
Concludes that expansion of small urban places may be the best spatial strategy for Kenya's development.

72-18 TEMPLE, FREDERICK T. 'Planning and budgeting for urban growth in Nairobi'. Journal of Eastern African Research and Development, 1973, pp. 191-216.
Discusses how the City Council attempts to cope with a soaring population.

8 - ECONOMIC STATISTICS

80 - General and macro-economic statistical publications

80-1 CRAIG, J. 'An East African import price index, 1954-1963, calculated from supplying countries' export indices'. EAER, June 1966, pp. 39-54.
Criticises the indices conventionally used and provides an alternative.

80-2 East African Common Services Organisation. The Balance of Payments of East Africa, 1959, 1960, and 1961. Government Printer, Nairobi, Sept. 1963, 30 pp.
The sixth report on East Africa's international economic transactions.

80-3 East African Statistical Department. East African Trade Indices: Revised External Trade Indices, 1954-61. Nairobi, Jan. 1963, 38 pp.
Presents improved series, overcoming past objections to a 1950 base year.

80-4 HAZLEWOOD, ARTHUR. 'Consistent trade statistics of Kenya, Uganda and Tanganyika for 1950 and earlier years'. Econ Stat Rev, Dec. 1973, pp. VIII-XXI.
Analyses the import and re-export statistics of the three countries between 1923 and 1950.

80-5 _____. 'Statistics of Kenya and Uganda imports, 1923-1948'. Econ Stat Rev, March 1973, pp. VIII-XXV.
Presents statistical series of imports and explains some pitfalls liable to trap the unwary user.

80-6 HIEBER, H. Uganda as an Example of (Statistics in) Developing Countries. Weltforum Verlag, Munich, 1969, 224 pp.
Discusses the state and improvement of economic statistics.

80-7 Kenya, Central Bureau of Statistics. 'Indices of inter-East African trade'. K Stat Dig, Sept. 1971, pp. 5-9.
Describes the methods used for unit value and quantum indices of exports and imports.

80-8 _____. Input/Output Table for Kenya, 1967. Government Printer, Nairobi, 1972, 9 pp.
Presents five 30 x 30 tables with a brief description of methodology and data sources.

80-9 _____. 'Stocks in the economy of Kenya, 1964-1968'. K Stat Dig, June 1969, pp. 1-4.
Presents inventory estimates for mining and quarrying; manufacturing and construction; electricity; commerce and agriculture.

80-10 LURY, D. A. 'The trade statistics of the countries of East Africa, 1945-1964'. Econ Stat Rev, March 1965, pp. 8-17.
Attempts to produce a consistent series of trade data for Kenya, Uganda and Tanganyika, including interterritorial trade.

80-11 McKEE, JANET W. Trade and Industrial Development. Mimeographed. IDS Miscellaneous Paper 86, July 1968, 93 pp.
A bibliography with statistics on trade and industrial development in Kenya.

80-12 OFSTAD, H. G. K. 'East African trade indices'. Econ Stat Rev, Sept. 1968, pp. VIII-XIV.

ECONOMIC STATISTICS

(OFSTAD, H. G. K.)
Presents revised methods used for calculating net import and domestic export indices.

80-13 POWELL, RAYMOND P. The Stock of Fixed Capital in Kenya, 1964-71. IDS Occasional Paper No. 9, 1973, 73 pp.
Presents and explains a general-purpose series relating to the monetary economy.

80-14 SAMUELS, L. H., ed. African Studies in Income and Wealth. Bowes, London, 1963, 432 pp.
Includes C. J. Martin, 'The development and diversity of national income series in East Africa since 1947'; T. A. Kennedy, H. W. Ord and D. Walker 'On the calculation and interpretation of national accounting material in East Africa'.

80-15 Tanzania, Bureau of Statistics. An Input-Output Table for Tanzania, 1969. Government Printer, Dar-es-Salaam, 1973, 9 pp.
Presents a 45 x 45 table for 1969, and describes methods used.

80-16 _____. National Accounts of Tanzania, 1964-1972. Mimeographed. Dar-es-Salaam, 1974, 69 pp.
Presents revised national accounts and describes methods employed in the revision.

80-17 _____. Prices and Price Index Numbers, June 1968-June 1969. Government Printer, Dar-es-Salaam, 1971, 81 pp.
Presents retail prices in shops and markets from eighteen towns in Tanzania, used to compute a national mainland consumer price index.

80-18 Uganda, Republic of. Report on the Balance of Payments of Uganda. D. G. Badger, Chairman. Government Printer, Entebbe, 1964, 30 pp.
Reviews existing estimates and concludes that the East African Statistical Department should retain its role as co-ordinator and principal tabulator of balance of payments information.

80-19 Uganda, Statistics Division. The Real Growth of the Economy of Uganda, 1954-62. Mimeographed. Entebbe, 1964, 50 pp.
Presents constant-price national accounts and describes methods used to deflate from current price series.

80-20 VAN ARKADIE, BRIAN. 'Gross domestic product estimates for East Africa'. Econ Stat Rev, Dec. 1963, pp. VIII-XIII.
Introduces the concepts used in East African accounts and compares the methods used in the three countries.

80-21 WEST, R. L. 'Estimates of national accounts for Kenya, 1923-1939'. EAER, Dec. 1965, pp. 23-45.
Presents national accounts estimates, with a discussion of sources and methods.

80-22 WOOD, G. D. 'Problems of comparisons in Africa with special regard to Kenya'. Review of Income and Wealth, March 1973, pp. 105-16.
Describes the data problems and other practical difficulties involved in attempting to make Kenyan statistics comparable with those of other countries, with special reference to incomes and purchasing power.

81 - Micro-economic statistical publications

81-1 BARTELMUS, P. and WALUGEMBE-MUSOKE, A. W. 'East African statistics of manufacturing activities, 1967-1969: methods and results'. Econ Stat Rev, Sept. 1973, pp. VIII-XXV.
Presents and describes a series of comparable statistics of East African manufacturing activities.

81-2 East African Community. East African Customs and Excise Tariffs. Customs and Excise Department, Arusha, July 1971, 162 pp.
Tariff rates for various items.

81-3 JENSEN, S. B. and MKAMA, J. District Data--Tanzania, 1967. Ministry of Economic Affairs and Development Planning, Dar-es-Salaam, 1968, 81 pp.
A statistical presentation, including data on population, employment, production, trade, income and value-added by district.

81-4 Kenya, Central Bureau of Statistics. Employment and Earnings in the Modern Sector, 1968-70. Government Printer, Nairobi, 1972, 129 pp.
Presents 3-digit level data on economic activity and tables on self-employed persons and family workers.

81-5 _____. 'A Kenya index of manufacturing production'. K Stat Dig, March 1964, pp. 2-3.
Presents an index indicating changes over time in the volume of goods produced, processed or repaired.

ECONOMIC STATISTICS

81-6 Kenya, Central Bureau of Statistics. 'Register of establishments in the Central Bureau of Statistics'. K Stat Dig, Sept. 1973, pp. 4-12.
Presents the scheme of classification used for the Bureau's register of establishments in the modern sector of the economy.

81-7 _____. 'Road vehicle statistics'. K Stat Dig, Dec. 1974, pp. 6-10.
Presents new data including registration, age, body type, and vehicle densities by Province.

81-8 _____. Migration and Tourism Statistics. Government Printer, Nairobi, 1974, 69 pp.
Statistical series on migration and tourism, 1968-71.

81-9 _____. 'Statistical application of "remote sensing"'. K Stat Dig, March 1975, pp. 1-2.
Discusses the potential of satellite imagery and aerial photography for temporal and spatial analysis of such topics as land use.

81-10 Tanzania, Bureau of Statistics. Survey of Distributive Trade, Dar-es-Salaam-1970. Mimeographed. Dar-es-Salaam, 1972, 31 pp.
Presents methodology and statistical results for 1970 relating to distributive establishments having at least one employee.

Index of Subjects and Places

Numbers refer to individual entries. The letters K, T and U indicate the country to which the entry refers; absence of a letter implies that the entry refers to more than one of the countries, or to East Africa as a whole.

Index of Authors, Editors and Chairmen

(Numbers refer to individual entries in the bibliography.)